☆LIFE IN THE☆
THIRD REICH

⚡LIFE IN THE⚡
THIRD REICH
DAILY LIFE IN NAZI GERMANY
1933-1945

PAUL ROLAND

ARCTURUS

ARCTURUS

This edition published in 2017 by Arcturus Publishing Limited
26/27 Bickels Yard, 151–153 Bermondsey Street,
London SE1 3HA

Typesetting by Palimpsest Book Production Limited
Cover image: courtesy of Bundesarchiv/Bild-146-1973-060-021/
o.Ang

ISBN: 978-1-78599-092-2
DA004560UK

Printed in China

Contents

Preface

When the Allies occupied a defeated Germany in the spring
of 1945 they shared a desire to mete out retribution to those
members of the Nazi leadership and their minions who had
brought so much suffering and destruction to the world
during five long years of war. This need was felt particularly
strongly by the Russians, who believed that they had suffered
the most from the barbarous cruelty handed out by Hitler's
forces in their crusade to subjugate the Slavic people and
eradicate the blight of communism from Eastern Europe.

The problem was that it was not so easy to identify the
middle- and lower-ranking Nazis once they had divested
themselves of their uniforms, destroyed all incriminating
documents and melted into the chaos of a disintegrated
society. In the ensuing confusion, justice was rough and
ready, frequently dispensed without due process by battle-
weary, sleep-deprived soldiers who were understandably
unforgiving and disinclined to adhere to the Geneva
Convention. It was not unknown for captured Nazi officers
who calmly enquired where they would be billeted to be

deliberately pointed in the direction of patrols with instructions to shoot enemy soldiers on sight.

Senior Allied officers had devised their own way of distinguishing Nazi sympathizers from the general population. They were confident that if they were approached by civilian officials eager to assure their liberators that they had not been loyal Nazis, the officers could be sure they had identified the very Nazis they were looking for and could promptly lock them up.

Although Hitler, Himmler and Goebbels had all committed suicide in the final days of the war and many senior-ranking SS officers had evaded justice via the so-called 'Vatican rat lines' to South America, the Allies had some success in delivering formal justice to those they held responsible for

Hitler, Goering and Goebbels and other high profile members of the Nazi leadership were familiar faces through newsreels and newspapers but other members of the regime would prove hard to identify and track down.

'waging aggressive war' and for initiating 'crimes against humanity'. They put 22 of the most notorious members of the Nazi leadership on public trial at Nuremberg in November 1945, among them Hermann Goering, Rudolf Hess, Joachim von Ribbentrop and Albert Speer. Martin Bormann, Hitler's private secretary, was tried and found guilty in absentia. His fate was the subject of much speculation for almost three decades until his remains were discovered not far from Hitler's Berlin bunker in 1972 and formally identified using genetic testing in 1998. The 23rd defendant, Robert Ley, had taken his own life before the trial began.

Behind closed doors, the judicial process had been fraught with unseemly squabbling between the Soviets and their former allies, who disagreed on many significant details. Overall, however, there was a belief that justice had been done and, more importantly, had been seen to be done. By the time subsequent trials had taken place of senior Nazi judges, members of the SS, a dozen or so extermination camp doctors and the most sadistic female concentration camp guards, the will to prosecute a vanquished enemy had given way to the desire to make the best of the peace that had been hard won and at such an enormous cost. Those Germans living in the west of their divided country were now allies of the European democracies, who were engaged in a Cold War with the Communist Bloc. The Soviet presence in East Germany and particularly in a partitioned Berlin was seen as a real and immediate threat to world peace. Consequently, Nazi hunting was left to amateurs such as Simon Wiesenthal, a Holocaust survivor who would not let the world forget that men such as Dr Josef Mengele and Adolf Eichmann were still at large.

Servicemen and women were impatient to go home and get on with their lives, and there was a general need to leave the horrors of the war in the past. Besides, there was a serious danger in presuming collective guilt when even the de-Nazification courts had identified three levels of 'offenders', distinguishing between the leadership, who would be indicted for 'waging aggressive war', and their subordinates accused of war crimes – as distinct from those deemed to be mere 'followers', who were unlikely to face prosecution. The process of de-Nazification was considered so large and complex that General Eisenhower estimated that it could take 50 years to purge Germany of Nazi ideology.

However, Germany's infrastructure and administration was in ruins, so pragmatism and realpolitik took precedence. In 1945, eight and a half million people – more than 10 per cent of the population – were still registered members of the Nazi party, with the highest proportion being civil servants, lawyers and teachers. As these individuals were needed to run basic services, their past was frequently overlooked. In the 1950s, it was estimated that 60 per cent of the civil servants in Bavaria were known to be former Nazis, but it was not until the 1960s that the next generation began asking awkward questions of their parents and querying the complacency of Konrad Adenauer's government regarding the prosecution of war criminals in the immediate post-war years.

The fact of the matter is that Hitler's Germany was not comprised of hard-core fanatics, with a small minority actively or passively opposed to the regime (the latter justifying their failure to act by citing the feeble defence known as 'internal emigration', a term coined by German writer Erich Kastner).

The defendants in the dock at Nuremberg, November 1945. Of the 22 former functionaries of the Nazi leadership on trial, only Goering retained any semblance of his once formidable personality.

Even among the most devout followers, there were those who 'had their reasons' for being converted to the Nazi cause. Fifteen-year-old Hilde Schlegel joined after attending an event organized by the party at which she tasted real buttered rolls for the first time and consequently believed that Hitler would ensure a better quality of life for the underprivileged. Some joined out of self-interest, seeking advancement; others for the reasons frequently cited by historians – the belief that the National Socialists would bring political stability, prosperity, employment and the return of territory seized under the hated Versailles Treaty.

But as this book will show, a sizeable proportion of Germany's citizens impassively witnessed the country's descent into dictatorship because they believed they were simply powerless to prevent it – as well as many more who could not see the danger until it was too late.

Chapter One
The Worst of Times

The Aftermath of 1918

'The confused locksmith Drexler provided the kernel, the drunken poet Eckart some of the "spiritual" foundation, the economic crank Feder what passed as an ideology, the homosexual Roehm the support of the Army and the war veterans, but it was now the former tramp, Adolf Hitler, not quite thirty-one and utterly unknown, who took the lead in building up what had been no more than a back-room debating society into what would soon become a formidable political party.'

(William L. Shirer on Hitler's takeover of the German Worker's Party in 1921)

The Nazis did not attract their initial supporters through persuasive political argument, nor by appealing to their ideals and aspirations, but by simply promising to provide for their immediate and fundamental needs – work and bread. Many who voted for them in the 1920s and even some of those who joined their ranks and marched under their banners during these early days of 'the struggle', sincerely and naively believed that National Socialism offered the only credible opposition to Bolshevism.

Not all of Hitler's early followers shared his virulent anti-Semitism, or subscribed to the more fanciful elements of his party's pseudo-völkisch ideology, which declared that the Germans were descendants of an Aryan master race and were destined to rule over inferior nations.

In the immediate aftermath of the country's defeat of November 1918, the population was weary, dispirited and looking for a leader with ready answers – someone who could identify those who were to blame for their misfortunes.

Defeat in November 1918 was seen as more than a military debacle. It brought humiliation to the German soldier who soon subscribed to the myth that the Army had been 'stabbed in the back' by defeatism generated at home by weak, defeatist politicians.

Families throughout the country were grieving for the incalculable loss of life, confounded by the sudden and unexpected capitulation of an army they had been assured was on the verge of victory, and embittered by the futility of the sacrifice they had made in vain for the Fatherland. This sense of despair was compounded by the abdication of the Kaiser and the new Weimar government's willing compliance with the punitive terms and conditions imposed by the Versailles Treaty. It is therefore no wonder that this poisonous atmosphere gave rise to extreme nationalism and the belief that the army had been betrayed, or 'stabbed in the back', to borrow a phrase attributed to General Ludendorff.

This grievous wound might have healed over time had it not been aggravated by the rampant inflation of 1922–3, which saw savings wiped out and wages devalued to the point where workers were being paid twice a day so that they could buy food while it was still affordable. Even so, it was not uncommon to see customers paying for produce with what had once been a month's wages, all of which emphasized the fragility of the economy and the ineffectiveness of the Weimar government. Within a year the average price of a loaf of bread had risen from 165 marks to one and a half million.

In every village, town and city, men, women and children could be seen begging for food and spare change, or asking for menial work of any kind. Into this desperate situation the Nazis appeared under the guise of the National Socialist German Workers' Party with a promise of jobs for the unemployed and relief for the impoverished. In addition, they declared their intention to purge commercial institutions of Jewish influence and to rid German business of 'unfair competition' (i.e. Jews). They vowed to crush the communists and put an end to the frequent and bloody skirmishes between rival political factions that made the streets unsafe for law-abiding citizens. They would also restore national pride by tearing up the hated Versailles Treaty and demanding the return of territory seized by the Allies after 1918. Every citizen was persuaded to believe it was his or her patriotic duty to vote for the programme. Hitler's critics accused him of being a crude, ill-educated rabble-rouser, but he articulated the people's anger and sense of injustice more effectively than the professional politicians and it was evident that he had touched a raw nerve.

'He was not easily discouraged. And he knew how to wait. As he picked up the threads of his life in the little two-room apartment on the top floor of 41 Thierschstrasse in Munich during the winter months of 1925 and then, when summer came, in various inns on the Obersalzberg above Berchtesgaden, the contemplation of the misfortunes of the immediate past and the eclipse of the present, served only to strengthen his resolve ... And there was born in him anew a burning sense of mission – for himself and for Germany – from which all doubts were excluded.'

(William L. Shirer on Hitler after his release from Landsberg Prison in December 1924, having served 264 days for planning the failed Munich Putsch [coup] the previous year.)

The Nazis' popularity rose and fell during the 1920s as the economy recovered then dipped again following the 1929 Wall Street Crash. But by 1933, the German people had lost their patience with their elected representatives and were prepared to set aside any concerns they might have had with

When inflation was at its height the German mark was of more value as fuel for the kitchen stove than as currency.

regard to the reported 'excesses' of the SA (the party's
brown-shirted enforcers) to give these untested newcomers
a chance.

However, there was nothing inevitable about the Nazis'
seizure of power. In the final parliamentary election before
Hitler was handed the chancellorship by the ageing President
Hindenburg in January 1933, the party suffered a significant
reversal of fortunes. Its share of the vote fell from 37 per
cent to 33, giving it fewer than 200 seats in the Reichstag –
just a third of the total. But Hitler's acolytes were certain that
it was only a matter of time before their day would come.

First Signs

*'As the year of 1931 ran its uneasy course, with five million
wage earners out of work, the middle classes facing ruin,
the farmers unable to meet their mortgage payments, the
Parliament paralyzed, the government floundering,
the eighty-four-year-old president fast sinking into the
befuddlement of senility, a confidence mounted in the
breasts of the Nazis.'*

(William L. Shirer, *The Rise and Fall of the Third Reich: A History of
Nazi Germany*)

For Berlin schoolboy Bernt Engelmann, the first indication
that there was something distinctly sinister lurking behind
the men in the brown shirts who had been pamphleteering
and making street corner speeches in his neighbourhood
came on a Monday morning in May 1932. It would be eight
months before Hitler became chancellor, but already there
were visible signs that his followers were impatient for

power. Someone had hoisted a large swastika flag from the roof of the secondary school in Wilmersdorf and it was attracting the attention of students and staff. One of the teachers ordered the janitor to take it down, but the man just grinned insolently and protested that he didn't have the key to the turret door. Several older students laughed at this and one remarked that if the hoisting of the flag was a sign that Hitler was already in power, then 'heads would roll', a notion that appeared to please the janitor.

Incensed, the teacher strode off to inform the principal, who was already on the phone protesting to the superintendent of schools, but before any action could be taken another teacher was seen to emerge from an upper window, clamber onto the roof with the nimbleness of a mountaineer and tear down the flag. This was greeted with much encouragement from the boys who had gathered in the yard and whose spontaneous applause drowned out the boos and hisses issued by their Nazi-loving classmates. The feat was all the more remarkable as it had been accomplished by the French master, Dr Levy, who had lost an arm in the Great War. But if the boys expected to be regaled with details of Dr Levy's exploits during that morning's class they were to be disappointed. Even after he had slid the blackboard up to write on a second slate panel underneath and had found the words *Salope Juif!* [Jewish Sow] scrawled in large letters, he remained calm and composed. He simply explained that the phrase showed an incorrect use of French grammar and that the more appropriate phrase was *Manchot Juif*, meaning a Jewish veteran.

Engelmann estimated that of the 450 pupils in his school about 40 had expressed Nazi sympathies. That morning they were inflamed with victory, the party having just won a majority in the regional election in Oldenburg, and the despised Chancellor Brüning had resigned. It would be only a matter of hours, they believed, until President Hindenburg appointed Hitler his successor. They would not take the insult of having their flag removed without a fight. During recess, three of the older boys marched into the principal's office to register a complaint against Dr Levy – two bore the uniform of the Hitler Youth and the third was in SA brown shirt, breeches and boots in defiance of a government ban on the wearing of paramilitary uniforms. Instead of calling the police, the principal placated them by promising to suspend Dr Levy until a full investigation could be held.

His capitulation was perceived by the Nazi bullies as permission to take their spite out on the Jewish students. Several ganged up on the younger boys, whom they beat mercilessly with their fists and belts until they bled. Engelmann witnessed several such incidents that morning. But the Nazis were not yet in power and there were still sufficient numbers of outraged parents to question the principal's handling of the affair. For all his talk of proceeding with 'utmost severity' against those seeking to politicize the school, Engelmann's parents had detected a note of sympathy in his voice towards the Nazis. It was just one example of what the American oral historian Studs Terkel called a lack of 'civil courage' and it could be argued that this form of cowardice was as much to blame for the rise of Hitler as the uncritical adoration heaped upon him by his supporters.

Not long after this incident, the Engelmann family moved to Düsseldorf, where Bernt attended a school that had not yet been infected by what he describes as the 'contagion of Nazi ideology'. He attributed his instinctive revulsion for rabid nationalism to the environment in which he grew up. His father was a staunch believer in democracy, his mother had offered practical assistance to the 'victims of an obviously inhuman policy' and his grandfather, a trade unionist, Social Democrat and confirmed pacifist, had advised the boy to join a Socialist Workers' youth group. Bernt's paternal grandmother also instilled in him a distrust of sabre-rattling militarism and the conservative aristocracy who, she said, regarded the top government posts as their birthright. But it was only when Bernt witnessed the public burning of books written by authors that he had read and admired that he realized the Nazis were the enemies of educated, free-thinking people such as himself.

Later, as a young man during the war, he joined a resistance group but was arrested by the Gestapo and interned in Flossenbürg and Dachau concentration camps. After Germany's capitulation, he became an eminent investigative journalist and returned to Berlin, where he interviewed many of the people with whom he'd grown up during the 1930s. He was shocked to discover that several of his former friends had highly selective memories of that period and that more than a few attributed their participation in the Hitler Youth to nothing more than 'youthful idealism'.

There was Marga, for example, a pretty, vivacious girl who recalled the thrill of the street parades with their flags and bunting and singing in the streets. She told him, 'All in all, we had a wonderful carefree youth, didn't we?'

Marga's father, a presiding judge of the district court and an ardent Nazi, had forbidden his wife from shopping at Jewish-owned stores and had been strict with their daughter, insisting that she be home every evening by 7 pm. But after the *Röhm Putsch* [the 'Night of the Long Knives'] on 30 June 1934, he had been a changed man. The news that Hitler had ordered the murder of more than 1,000 people without trial (some of whom were silenced to prevent them revealing details of his past) had left the judge disillusioned and seriously questioning his allegiance to the party. He no longer objected to his wife shopping at Jewish-owned stores. Nor did he seem to care what time his daughter came home. It appears that one of his friends, the music critic Dr Wilhelm Schmid, had been murdered on the Night of the Long Knives by four SS men, who had dragged him from his apartment and shot him in the mistaken belief that he was the SA leader Willi Schmidt.

Marga hadn't thought to ask her father or mother why her father had changed and it was only two years later, after she had married, that he spoke about it.

All Marga could recall were the popular songs of the time, the balls she had attended and the films she had seen. She remembered the first time she and Bernt had been to the theatre to see a performance of Friedrich Schiller's *Don Carlos* and could still recall the names of the cast, but she had no idea why members of the audience had broken into spontaneous applause during a scene in which one of the characters implores his employer, 'Sire, grant us freedom of thought', until Bernt explained it had been to demonstrate their opposition to the regime's suppression of free speech.

It was experiences such as these that led Engelmann to conclude that the Nazification of his country was neither the work of 'sinister demons' nor the inevitable result of 'grim fate' for which no one could be held accountable, but simple self-interest and timidity.

Hearts and Minds

The Nazis had made a concerted effort to win over the hearts and minds of the population, ingratiating themselves with every section of German society and making promises they had no intention of keeping. They had also mastered the art of political propaganda by staging mass rallies and marches that emphasized their unity and fanaticism but which gave a false impression of their popularity. Their campaign to win the state of Lippe in the January 1933 parliamentary election was typical.

Unless they won this marginal state and made up for the serious reverses they had suffered throughout the country in the November 1932 Reichstag elections, it was feared that the industrialists and bankers would withdraw their financial support and the party would give in to factional infighting and eventually destroy itself. Consequently, Hitler and Goebbels mounted a sustained campaign using the last reserves of party funds and every publicity stunt they could conceive of to secure the votes of the 100,000 inhabitants.

Over ten days they staged 900 events, with Hitler delivering speeches at 16 major rallies. Thousands of SA and SS men were drafted in to march through the streets of every town and village in the region, shouting slogans and putting on a show of strength while cars equipped with loudspeakers urged the population to vote. It created the impression that the party was not only substantial and well funded but also very popular. In fact, despite all of their parades and pageantry, they managed to increase their share of the vote by only 6,000.

The democratic parties won a total of 50,000 votes between them to the Nazis' 39,000, but the right-wing ultra-nationalist press hailed it as a significant victory and a fortnight later President Hindenburg was persuaded to appoint Hitler the new chancellor.

A Better Class of People

'In the summer of 1933 … any collective resistance had become impossible; individual resistance was merely another form of suicide.'
(Sebastien Haffner, quoted in *German Voices* by Professor Frederic C. Tubach)

Horst Kruger, the teenage son of a Berlin civil servant, witnessed the euphoria that greeted Hitler's accession to the chancellorship in 1933:

'It was a cold night in January and there was a torchlight parade. The radio announcer, whose resonant tones were closer to singing and sobbing than reporting, was experiencing ineffable events … something about Germany's reawakening, and always adding as a refrain that now everything, everything would be different and better … The time was ripe … a surge of greatness seemed to course through our country...'

That week it looked as if every house and business in the quiet suburb of Eichkamp had hung out swastika flags and even children's bicycles were adorned with a fluttering pennant, many of them handmade by the parents because the manufacturers couldn't cope with the demand. Horst's parents had not shared their friends and neighbours'

The Führer became the centre of a personality cult, which saw him mobbed by adoring followers at his many carefully stage-managed personal appearances.

enthusiasm for the new administration, but they were quietly hopeful that it signalled an end to the economic uncertainty that had hung over the country in the past few years and that it might stop the outbursts of violence between rival political groups. So they joined in with the celebrations, if only to show their willingness to give the Nazis a go and also to demonstrate their good will and sense of community.

'Suddenly one was a somebody,' Horst recalled, 'part of a better class of people, on a higher level – a German.'

Everybody was included. At least everyone who was an ethnic German. But even many Jews hoped that the anti-Semitic frenzy they had suffered might die down now that the party was in power and that its extreme elements might be reined in, if only to quell criticism in the foreign press. Private anxieties were put on hold for the duration while the country turned out en masse for what seemed at the time to be a series of endless parades and processions. The jubilant atmosphere was heightened with the announcement of new holidays celebrating various aspects of German life and culture, and when the extensive programme of public works was announced, the excitement escalated. The misery of crippling unemployment and economic depression appeared to have been erased at a stroke. People were buoyant, optimistic and alive with a sense of purpose. Members of the Labour Service marched through the streets with spades slung over their shoulders on their way to lay the foundations for a new Germany that would be connected by an extensive network of autobahns. But after the new art galleries and government ministries had been built on a grand scale, the rundown tenements and slums remained and the same people who had waved their flags and cheered the processions consoled themselves with the thought that Hitler could not work miracles overnight. They would have to be patient.

And when it was announced that the SA had been purged of its more unruly elements in order to supress a counter-revolution, these same voices asked themselves if Hitler could have known about it and that, even if he had, he would surely not have approved of such barbarity.

Horst recalls that his neighbours were galvanized with a sense of national pride and excited at the prospect of being part of a more productive and prosperous nation. Bierkellers were packed with men holding forth on every aspect of government policy, from the reclaiming of territory occupied by the Allies to the benefits of the autobahn. They were under the impression that they would have a say in both international and local affairs, and soon became 'disarmed, willing and docile', consenting to anything the new administration cared to ask them to endorse through the ballot box. While the men boasted of standing up to the League of Nations as if it were a disagreeable neighbour, their wives discussed the possibility of having or adopting children to fulfil their maternal duty to the Fatherland.

With each new territorial acquisition, Hitler's reputation as a statesman increased tenfold. To have achieved such significant and substantial gains without embroiling the country in a war and in the face of international condemnation seemed to confirm that the Führer had been sent by God to reclaim what was Germany's by right. His ardent admirers began to snip his speeches out of the newspapers so they could discuss them with their family and friends as they might once have debated the Sunday sermon. Horst's mother was typical, he says, of those who 'lived on

Hitler was venerated throughout the Reich as a saviour sent by God to restore national pride and recover territory occupied by the victorious allies after the First World War.

illusions'. A devout Catholic, she saw Hitler as the penniless artist who had risen above his lowly origins to restore Germany to its rightful place on the world stage and whose faith would inspire him to make the well-being of the people his priority. The Führer, she assured her son, would not lie to his people.

Horst considered his neighbours to be 'honest believers, enthusiasts, inebriates' who had convinced themselves that life would be better under Hitler and who hoped that talk of war was no more than malicious rumours. Hitler did not want war, they told themselves – but when it came, many realized that Hitler had not only conquered Europe, he had also subjugated his own people. They existed merely to serve him.

Nazification

The administration's first proclamation was drafted to reassure the people of its reactionary credentials.

'The new national government will consider its first and supreme duty to restore our nation's unity of will and spirit. It will safeguard and defend the foundation on which the strength of our nation rests. It will firmly protect Christianity, the basis of our entire morality, it will safeguard the family … It wants to base the education of Germany's youth on a reverence for our great past, on pride in our old traditions. It will thus declare war on spiritual, political and cultural nihilism … the government will once again make national discipline our guide.'
(Adolf Hitler, 1 February 1933)

The Nazi leadership sought to cultivate an image of themselves as the architects of a new classless society in which employers were expected to take their meals with their employees and professionals worked side by side with the unqualified in state-regulated organizations such as the Labour Front. They also advocated unrestricted access to the universities and military academies for loyal party members, something that had previously been a privilege enjoyed only by the aristocracy and ruling elite. A limit was introduced, however, for female students enrolling in university, amounting to no more than 10 per cent of the total.

Hitler had prohibited women from taking an active role in politics and the professions, although he permitted them to work as unpaid activists drumming up support for the party and caring for its underprivileged members. Their natural place in the National Socialist state was to be selfless mothers of blond, blue-eyed Aryan babies, a role encapsulated in the party slogan *Kinder, Küche und Kirche* [Children, Kitchen and Church].

'The National Socialist revolution,' Hitler proclaimed, 'would be an entirely male event.' Nevertheless, 34,000 middle-class, middle-aged housewives had joined the party by 1933 – women such as Gertrud Scholtz-Klink, nominal figurehead of the Nazi Women's Union, whose fanatical loyalty earned her the nickname 'the Female Führer'; Elsbeth Zander, founder of the Order of the Red Swastika; Elizabeth Polster, who increased the membership of the National Socialist Women's Organization (NSF) by persuading her 66,500 members that Christianity and National Socialism were not mutually exclusive; and Guida Diehl, whose Nationalist Newland Movement predated the founding of the Nazi party by five years.

Gertrud Scholtz-Klink was the nominal leader of the German Women's Union, which claimed to have more than 6 million devoted followers but had no influence on policy. She was known as 'The Female Führer'.

As for unmarried single women, they were regarded as second-class citizens or *Staatsangehöriger* [subjects of the state], and afforded the same legal status as Jews and mentally disabled people. And yet, a significant proportion of Hitler's most ardent supporters were women, although it is a myth that they voted in greater numbers for the Nazis than for rival parties.

In practice, Hitler's inner circle paid only lip service to the principles of National Socialism. In private, Goebbels, Goering and their cohorts indulged to excess in their magnificent private villas while their wives flaunted their Paris fashions and cosmetics in defiance of their Führer, who had declared such luxuries to be ostentatious, vulgar and unpatriotic. Only Frau Bormann cultivated the dowdy peasant look that her Führer considered to be the image of the ideal German mother. She dressed in Tracht [heritage clothing] as dictated by the Reich Fashion Institute, braided her hair in a bun and declined to wear lipstick in the belief that it was made from animal fat, as Hitler had stated. Every year for ten years she dutifully bore another child.

Devoted to the Cause

Those who volunteered for local party activities invariably found that there was scant reward or acknowledgement for all the time and energy that they had devoted to the cause.

Typically, members of the Nazi Women's League would be put to work collecting dues and contributions to party funds, applying to various offices and agencies responsible for housing large families whom the party had promised to help; later they would assist with rehousing those who had been bombed out of their homes. Every free moment they could spare would be devoted to party projects of one sort or another and their only recognition would be a front seat at various local events, or perhaps the honour of presenting a bouquet to party officials, maybe even the Führer himself. These women, by all accounts, rarely complained and also remained staunchly loyal even after they were forced to face the horrors perpetrated by the regime.

More often than not they would blame Heinrich Himmler or other Nazi leaders but rarely Hitler, whom they believed shared their concern for the welfare of the German people. They dismissed the rumours regarding the extermination camps and atrocities committed by the SS in the conquered territories as malicious gossip. At party meetings they swallowed the official line – that the concentration camps had been built to imprison criminals, profiteers and other undesirable individuals who would be taught discipline and re-educated. The newspapers regularly reported details of those who had been arrested and what crime they had committed against the state to merit their subsequent internment, or execution. This made a mockery of their claim after the war that they knew nothing of what took place at camps within Germany, such as Dachau near Munich and Ravensbrück, north of Berlin. Such measures were generally considered necessary and it was understood that the inmates deserved to be dealt with severely. To enforce the impression that only habitual offenders were imprisoned in camps within Germany, the press printed photographs of individuals specially selected for their 'repulsive' appearance.

It was in the regime's interest to publicize the existence of the camps to act as a deterrent and this gave rise to the saying, 'Hush! Watch out! You don't want to end up in a concentration camp.'

Alignment

It was shortly after Hitler's appointment to the chancellorship that the new administration implemented the policy they called *Gleichschaltung* [bringing into line], which forced all institutions and various aspects of social and political life to conform to and adopt Nazi ideology. It began with a clampdown on Catholic youth organizations, the banning of Catholic publications, the closure of Catholic hospitals and schools and the imprisonment of the clergy, accused of decadence by Nazi publications such as *Der Stürmer* and *Das Schwarze Korps*. The regime also outlawed the Catholic Centre Party along with all opposition parties and removed many Catholics from civil-service posts.

Even high school students were obliged to sign a declaration of allegiance to the new regime in 1933. Helene Jacobs refused and was consequently barred from taking her final exams. On leaving school she found poorly paid employment with a Jewish attorney, but believing that the Nazis would soon be forced out of office she was determined to stick to her principles. She considered the whole idea of an Aryan master race to be contrary to everything that she had been taught and was determined to express her disapproval:

'The point that aroused me from the beginning was that we as a people had to show our unwillingness in some fashion, not just when the crimes began, but before, when it started, with this so-called "Aryan" ancestry. They distributed questionnaires and you had to say whether you had "Aryan" ancestors. Everyone filled them out. I said, "We can't go along with this; it's not legal. We must do something against this and throw the questionnaires away." But today – the other people my age, they behaved totally differently at that time. Most of them built their careers then. When I said, "I'm not going to have anything to do with this," I isolated myself.'

(Victoria Barnett, *For the Soul of the People*)

Gleichschaltung was not confined to state schools. Universities too were infiltrated by the New Order's enforcers.

Peter Drucker, a Frankfurt University lecturer, hoped that he might be able to remain in his post but was shocked by what he witnessed during the first Nazified faculty meeting held just weeks after Hitler had become chancellor:

'Frankfurt was the first university the Nazis tackled, precisely because it was the most self-confidently liberal of major German universities, with a faculty that prided itself on its allegiance to scholarship, freedom of conscience and democracy. The Nazis therefore knew that control of Frankfurt University would mean control of German academia. And so did everyone at the university. Above all, Frankfurt had a science faculty distinguished both by its scholarship and by its liberal convictions; and outstanding among the Frankfurt scientists was a biochemist–physiologist of Nobel-Prize calibre and impeccable liberal credentials.'

Drucker had never thought it necessary to attend a faculty meeting, but when a Nazi commissar for Frankfurt was appointed in the spring of 1933, he hoped that his pronouncements would provoke a reaction from the faculty members that would force the Nazis to back down and respect the university's autonomy.

'The new Nazi commissar wasted no time on the amenities. He immediately announced that Jews would be forbidden to enter university premises and would be dismissed without salary on March 15; this was something no one had thought possible despite the Nazis' loud anti-Semitism. Then he launched into a tirade of abuse, filth, and four-letter words such as had been heard rarely

even in the barracks and never before in academia. He pointed his finger at one department chairman after another and said, "You either do what I tell you or we'll put you into a concentration camp." There was silence when he finished; everybody waited for the distinguished biochemist–physiologist. The great liberal got up, cleared his throat, and said, "Very interesting, Mr Commissar, and in some respects very illuminating: but one point I didn't get too clearly. Will there be more money for research in physiology?" The meeting broke up shortly thereafter with the commissar assuring the scholars that indeed there would be plenty of money for "racially pure science". A few of the professors had the courage to walk out with their Jewish colleagues, but most kept a safe distance from these men who only a few hours earlier had been their close friends. I went out sick unto death – and I knew that I was going to leave Germany within forty-eight hours.'

An anonymous college professor excused his support for the New Order in a conversation with American academic Milton Mayer after the war by explaining that he had been swept along by the surge of enthusiasm for the new administration and what promised to be a new era of study and scholarship.

'Middle High German was my life. It was all I cared about. I was a scholar, a specialist. Then, suddenly, I was plunged into all the new activity, as the university was drawn into the new situation; meetings, conferences, interviews, ceremonies, and, above all, papers to be filled out, reports, bibliographies, lists, questionnaires. And on top of that were

*demands in the community, the things in which one had to,
was "expected to" participate, that had not been there or
had not been important before. It was all rigmarole, of
course, but it consumed all one's energies, coming on top of
the work one really wanted to do. You can see how easy it
was, then, not to think about fundamental things. One had
no time. Too Busy to Think.'*

The professor admitted that the new routine, the continuous
changes and crisis engineered by the regime:

*'... provided an excuse not to think for people who did
not want to think anyway ... Most of us did not want to
think about fundamental things and never had.
There was no need to.'*

The ever-present threat posed by enemies within and
without distracted 'decent' people from considering the
consequences of what they were participating in, until it was
too late to do anything.

*'Suddenly it all comes down, all at once. You see what you
are, what you have done, or, more accurately, what you
haven't done (for that was all that was required of most of
us: that we do nothing). You remember those early meetings
of your department in the university when, if one had stood,
others would have stood, perhaps, but no one stood. A small
matter, a matter of hiring this man or that, and you hired
this one rather than that. You remember everything now,
and your heart breaks. Too late. You are compromised
beyond repair.'*

(Milton Mayer, *They Thought They were Free*)

Working Under the Nazis

But the Nazis did not manage to intimidate everyone. Less fanatical party members might overlook critical remarks said in their presence by friends, while some even went so far as to warn communist colleagues of an imminent wave of arrests. This was especially true among manual workers in the factories, shipyards and on the railways, where comradeship often came before party loyalty. The suspect could then lie low for a few days and their absence could be blamed on a bout of illness. But many political opponents of the regime were not so fortunate. Anyone could be sacked on the spot without reason, although the official pretext for their dismissal would be put down to 'political unreliability'.

Skilled workers tended to be better informed about their rights and valued their unions, which the Nazis abolished as soon as they seized power. These men felt aggrieved that the regime now forbade them any say in working conditions and excluded them from wage negotiations. They resented the fact that Hitler had established Labour Trustees and that he had authorized these to set wages that were often agreed behind closed doors with management.

Manual labourers and white-collar workers were also acutely aware that their wages declined steadily during the Nazi era, while income from factory ownership and investment rose. Workers found themselves putting in longer hours and working faster to meet production targets in the hope of receiving an increase in wages.

While the Nazi leadership declared their solidarity with the people, they enacted laws that bound workers to a form of medieval serfdom. Under the Law for the

Organization of National Labour (passed in 1934), for example, industry regressed to a feudal system with employees reduced to the status of servants. If an employer didn't want an employee to leave, they could refuse to hand over the documents that were required whenever someone began a new job.

The regime attempted to appease the workers and get the most out of them by initiating a programme they called *Kraft durch Freude* [strength through joy], which offered incentives to productivity in the form of holidays and state-subsidized leisure activities. By 1937, almost 38.5 million Germans had participated in these state-sponsored leisure activities, which included symphony concerts, theatre performances, cruises to Scandinavia and Spain and breaks to the German countryside.

It all sounded too good to be true and it was. The beneficiaries of these bonuses were often the highly skilled workers, administrative staff and management.

One branch of Robert Ley's organization promoted the building of leisure facilities and canteens in factories and offices, which employees were shocked to learn they would have to build and pay for themselves.

But the most cynical strategy was the offer of a Volkswagen car, which workers paid for over several years but that was never produced. Every employee who signed up for the scheme had 5 marks a month deducted from his or her wage packet in addition to taxes and compulsory contributions to Nazi welfare organizations. After three-quarters of the price had been paid, the employee would receive a voucher with an order number. They were never told, however, that the factory built to assemble the cars had been converted for the production of munitions.

Nazism insinuated itself into every aspect of its citizens' lives. This was not a burden for those who believed that life would get better under Hitler's leadership.

Undermining the Family

*'The National Reich Church of Germany categorically claims
the exclusive right and the exclusive power
to control all churches within the borders of the Reich:
it declares these to be national churches of the
German Reich.'*

(William L. Shirer, *The Nightmare Years*)

A more subtle and insidious tactic was for the regime to portray itself as the people's protector and benefactor, while at the same time usurping parental influence and undermining the authority of organized religion.

This process was formalized by the Enabling Act passed just one week after the burning of the Reichstag on 27 February 1933 – which is generally believed to have been planned and executed by the Nazis, who needed a pretext to persuade President Hindenburg to pass an emergency decree suspending civil rights. The act was blamed on a lone Dutch communist with learning difficulties, Marinus van der Lubbe, who was tried and summarily executed after a show trial. He was the first of 12,000 civilians to be eliminated by Nazi 'special courts' during the Third Reich (see: Peter Hoffmann, *The History of the German Resistance 1933–1945*).

Once the dictatorship had tightened its stranglehold on all government administrative offices and public institutions, it sought to insinuate itself in every aspect of its citizens' public and private lives. In May 1933 all trade unions were abolished and workers' rights were regulated by the Labour Front. The family was infected by Nazi ideology, which indoctrinated children, turning them against their parents, and attempts were made to supplant religion with a neo-pagan

form of worship that deified Hitler as the saviour of
the nation.

Hitler repeatedly stressed the role Christianity would play in
the National Socialist state while at the same time promoting
specious Nazi ideology that was in direct contradiction of
Church doctrine. It required that marriages and funerals be
formalized as neo-pagan ceremonies, with the swastika
replacing the crucifix on the altar, the Bible substituted by
Mein Kampf and prayers replaced with an oath of allegiance
to the head of state.

For a time, many regular churchgoers couldn't understand
why their pastors were censuring the new administration in
their weekly sermons when conditions had improved signifi-
cantly for the average working family. But then the book
burnings began, followed by concerted attempts to challenge
the authority of the Church and its clerics' objections to the
systematic elimination of those individuals who were deemed
to be of no value to the state.

Book Burning

On 10 May 1933, students in Berlin and other major
German cities organized the public burning of books
deemed to be 'un-German'. These included titles by Thomas
Mann, H. G. Wells, Jack London, Sigmund Freud, Albert
Einstein and the blind American author and political activist
Helen Keller. Propaganda minister Josef Goebbels had
incited the students of Berlin with a rabble-rousing speech
that betrayed the real reason for this act of intellectual
vandalism: the Nazis feared anything that encouraged the

masses to think for themselves and to question the validity of whatever they were told:

> '...The era of extreme Jewish intellectualism is now at an end ... The future German man will not just be a man of books, but a man of character. It is to this end that we want to educate you. As a young person, to already have the courage to face the pitiless glare, to overcome the fear of death, and to regain respect for death – this is the task of this young generation. And thus you do well in this midnight hour to commit to the flames the evil spirit of the past. This is a strong, great and symbolic deed...'

Bernt Engelmann witnessed the public burning of books written by authors that he had read and admired and realized that the Nazis were the enemies of educated, free-thinking people like himself. Nazism signalled not a political revolution but a return to barbarism.

The burnings provoked outrage around the world. Keller's book *How I Became a Socialist* was among the books hurled on the pyre. In an open letter to the student body of Germany, she expressed the ire and alarm that many artists and intellectuals felt on reading the reports of that night's events:

'History has taught you nothing if you think you can kill ideas. Tyrants have tried to do that often before, and the ideas have risen up in their might and destroyed them.

'You can burn my books and the books of the best minds in Europe, but the ideas in them have seeped through a million channels and will continue to quicken other minds. I gave all the royalties of my books for all time to the German soldiers blinded in the World War with no thought in my heart but love and compassion for the German people.

'I acknowledge the grievous complications that have led to your intolerance; all the more do I deplore the injustice and unwisdom of passing on to unborn generations the stigma of your deeds.'

A hundred years earlier the German–Jewish poet Heinrich Heine had written, 'Where one burns books, human beings will inevitably follow.'

Chapter Two
The New Order

Myth of the Economic Miracle

'The big businessmen, pleased with the new government that was going to put the organized workers in their place and leave management to run its businesses as it wished, were asked to cough up. This they agreed to do at a meeting on February 20 at Goering's Reichstag President's Palace, at which Dr Schacht acted as host and Goering and Hitler laid down the line to a couple of dozen of Germany's leading magnates, including Krupp von Bohlen, who had become an enthusiastic Nazi overnight, Bosch and Schnitzler of I.G. Farben, and Voegler, head of the United Steel Works. The record of this secret meeting has been preserved.'
(William L. Shirer, *The Rise and Fall of the Third Reich: A History of Nazi Germany*)

The population was indoctrinated with the lie that Hitler's public works programme, such as the building of the autobahn and the construction of the Siegfried Line (the defensive line known by Germans as the Westwall), had reduced unemployment, but it took the dictatorship almost four years – until 1936 – to bring unemployment down to an acceptable level. By that time the other industrial nations had recovered from the Great Depression and had done so without drafting every able-bodied man into the army and their less able brethren into the munitions factories.

The 'economic miracle' that Hitler is credited with achieving in Germany was attained at considerable cost. The majority of men who were drafted in to build the autobahns had to live on wages that were lower than their unemployment benefit. They were paid 51 pfennigs an hour compared to 66 pfennigs for comparable work in a factory or printing shop and they were compelled to work in the open air regardless of the weather. To add to their misery, they were required to live far from home in barracks where the conditions were on a par with prison and for which

Women workers fared worse than their male colleagues and were typically paid a third less as well as having to pay for their own travel to a workplace chosen for them by the state.

they were required to pay 15 pfennigs a day plus another 35 pfennigs for slop ladled out of a cauldron. The average weekly wage for these manual labourers was 16 marks a week after these compulsory 'contributions' had been deducted and they were rewarded with just ten days' holiday per year.

Many women were conscripted into factories and required to work 12-hour shifts.

Female workers fared even worse as they were not regarded as being of equal value. They were typically paid a third less than their male colleagues. A skilled female factory worker could expect to earn 35 marks a week with overtime, but from this she would have to deduct money for food supplied by the company and pay for her travel. Those who had been used to working a shift that allowed them to do their domestic chores before work now found themselves reporting to munitions factories or other branches of compulsory service as early as 6 am. If they lived far from the factory they would have to allow extra time for travelling, which meant that they could return home after a 12-hour shift to find most of the shops shut and those that remained open late with little fresh produce left to sell.

To add to their hardship, they would be too tired to take on the extra jobs such as office cleaning that might have earned them a few more marks a week. After paying for food and travel, many workers were left with just 10 marks a week. It was no wonder that the older women often suffered illness and fatigue, which increased dramatically with the onset of war, when Allied air raids frayed their nerves and deprived them of sleep.

Unemployment had been reduced from six million when Hitler came to power in 1933 to a third of that in just three years. However, the economy had suffered as a result because public works programmes had been financed by demanding that should banks issue massive loans, which wouldn't have been offered to a democratic government or private industry. The problem was compounded by the administration which printed the money required to pay for the loans. This would almost certainly have created hyperinflation had Germany not gone to war in 1939. But that had been Hitler's plan all along: he mobilized the population and increased the production of arms and munitions in order to wage war, not to create full employment or benefit the economy.

Shopkeepers and the owners of small businesses were another group who discovered that the party's election promises were no guarantee that their lot would improve under National Socialism. The Nazis had threatened to 'Aryanize' Jewish-owned department stores and firms that had been blamed for squeezing small traders and entrepreneurs out of business by buying in bulk and selling below the price their competitors could afford. But as soon as the Nazis had forced the Jewish businessmen out, they replaced them with Germans – some of whom proved even more ruthless when it came to cutting prices. The department stores remained open but under new German ownership and these men frequently refused to rent out units to small stallholders, something the previous owners had done. Many small businesses which had been holding out in the hope that the Nazis would create prosperity were forced to close, the victims of declining sales and customers who insisted on buying on credit because they couldn't pay outright for their goods.

Those whose shops and businesses struggled to remain profitable in the years before the war could appeal to their local *Kreisleiter* [block warden] to put in a word for them at local party headquarters, but frequently they were simply told to be patient, that Hitler couldn't perform miracles overnight and had to be given time for his economic programmes to take effect. When another year passed without any sign of improvement in trade, they might petition the *Kreisleiter* again, who would have been told by local party officials to advise the owners to sell out to the bigger stores or close their businesses and seek employment with the army. In the meantime, they could earn a little by selling subscriptions to the party newspaper, the *Völkischer Beobachter*, and collecting on behalf of the Winter Aid – although they themselves were probably in greater need of charity than the poor for whom they were collecting.

Chapter Two

Hitler's Children

The basic facilities that we take for granted today were considered luxuries for many German working-class families in the 1920s and 1930s.

BDM [*Bund Deutscher Mädel*; League of German Girls] member Ursula Dickreuther remembered having to wash without hot water in their unheated city apartment block, even in the bitterest winter. Her family had to resort to filling hot water bottles and heating them on the stove to take the chill off their beds. If they were lucky, the water might still be lukewarm by the morning, when they would empty the contents into a basin to wash themselves.

There were communal bathrooms in most apartment blocks, so tenants had to take turns and agree on a rota with the other residents. Public bathhouses offered showers for 50 pfennigs or a bath for 1 mark, but the larger families would make do as best they could at home to save even a few marks. Bath day saw all of the children washed in the same wooden laundry tub, one after the other, with the youngest having the first dip and the eldest the last. All of them used the same water topped up with buckets of scalding-hot water heated on the stove. Dishes, too, were washed in water heated on the stove and afterwards the buckets had to be scrubbed with Vim to remove the grimy ring. Clothes were also washed by hand with a washboard and a hard bristle brush, but often only once a month, and the wet laundry would be hung up inside the apartment unless the weather was good. Laundry day was loathed by children as it was the day when their mother was too busy to make food, so they had to make do with soup and bread – if they could afford it.

As so many families were forced to share facilities it was

common to rely on chamber pots, which had to be emptied every morning. With no toilet paper, people were forced to use pieces of newspaper strung on a wire in the communal bathroom. Such hardship had its positive side, though. Ursula believes that it was her habit of reading these cuttings that gave her a head start with her education.

Under the Nazis, education became synonymous with indoctrination. Spurious racial theories were taught to children from the age of six and textbooks were liberally sprinkled with quotes from *Mein Kampf*.

Children born to working-class German families in the interwar years experienced much the same level of hardship as their equivalent in other European countries. They were expected to do their share of the chores, fetching coal and firewood, running errands, even sweeping, scrubbing and waxing floors, beating rugs and polishing brass door fittings until they could see their faces in them.

But when their tasks were done they could run freely in the streets, ride their bikes or scooters or have fun on roller skates, if they had any. All but the most basic toys and board games were too expensive for the average working family at that time, so children relied on popular street games that needed only a skipping rope, a ball or a piece of chalk. If they had none of these, then it was hide and seek, tag or cowboys and Indians.

Entertainment was limited to a rare trip to the circus, cinema, fair or theatre. Only the middle class could afford to go swimming in the municipal baths; everyone else had to wait for the warmer weather and make do with the local river or lake. But winter brought the excitement of sledging (you needed only a tray and some string to steer it with), ice skating (with or without skates) and of course snowball fights.

Euthanasia

For those suffering from a disability, life under the Nazis was to prove unspeakably cruel. It started when compulsory sterilization for blind, deaf and physically disabled people, and for those suffering from chronic depression, was legalized in 1933 with the passing of the Law for the Prevention of Hereditarily Diseased Offspring. Even chronic alcoholism was deemed to be sufficient grounds for treatment.

Two years later, the Law for the Protection of the Hereditary Health of the German People was enacted. This forbade German citizens with hereditary or infectious diseases from marrying and producing 'sick and asocial offspring' who would be expected to become a 'burden on the community'.

Over the following four years, 200,000 compulsory sterilizations were performed and an efficient system was put in place to implement the administration's euthanasia programme.

Gerda Bernhardt's mentally disabled brother Manfred was one of 5,000 children murdered by Nazi physicians on the Führer's whim. There was no official order as such, only a *Führerstaat* [directive] that had apparently originated with a casual remark made by Hitler to his personal physician, Dr Karl Brandt, concerning the merits of killing those 'unworthy of life'.

Gerda recalled:

'Manfred was a lovely boy, but he could only say "Mama" and "Papa" ... He only learnt to walk very late too. He always liked to be busy. If my mother said, "bring some coal up from the cellar", he wanted to do it over and over again. My father was in favour of putting him in some sort of children's hospital and then Aplerbeck came up as they had a big farm there and the boy might be kept occupied.'

Aplerbeck had been established as a 'Special Children's Unit' where patients would be given a lethal injection and their parents informed that they had died of natural causes.

Gerda recalls the last time she saw her brother alive. 'They brought the boy into the waiting room. There was an orderly there when I was leaving. The boy stood at the window and I waved and waved and he waved too. That was the last time I saw him.'

Indoctrinating the Young

Long before the Nazis came to power, Hitler had declared the education of Germany's children to be a priority, but after 1933, when state schools came under the control of the dictatorship, it became clear that it was not education that Hitler had in mind but indoctrination. Racial ideology and the spurious pseudo-sciences replaced traditional subjects such as biology and history.

Even maths was used to disseminate Nazi propaganda, with pupils being asked, for example, how many marriage loans of 1,000 marks could be paid out to worthy Aryan couples if the 300,000 mentally ill people in care at the cost of 4 marks a day could be eliminated. Teachers were required to sanction the new curriculum and to prove their loyalty to the party by joining the Nazi Teachers' Association – 97 per cent did so. The remainder were forced to leave their posts. One third of female teachers had been compelled to take early 'retirement' in the year Hitler came to power in order to fulfil their primary role as homemakers and mothers.

Both primary and secondary teachers were predominantly male and were required to attend political education classes and to refute their former political allegiances. But even after their training was completed, they were informed that their performance would be monitored by their own pupils. Any infringements, deviations or disloyal remarks would be reported to the Federal Ministry of Education, whose remit was to ensure that all schools, universities and research institutes conformed to National Socialist ideology.

In *Mein Kampf* Hitler stated that the purpose of education was to prepare girls for motherhood and boys for the military.

A 1936/37 issue of Nazi women's magazine *Frauen Warte* itemized the educational principles of the New Germany:

> **Race**: National Socialist education means instruction in the ideas of the German people, in understanding German traditions, in arousing the pure, uncorrupted, and honourable people's consciousness, their sense of belonging to the community. Only an uncorrupted member of the German race can have such an understanding of his people, completing it with the willingness to sacrifice all for the nation.
>
> **Military training**: It is clear that the German youth must be determined to defend their Fatherland with their lives. Despite all the noise regarding promises and

disarmament, Germany is surrounded by enemies. The German youth must acquire military virtues. Their bodies must be hardened, made tough and strong, so that the youth may become efficient soldiers who are healthy, resilient, trained, vigorous and able to endure hardships.

Leadership: A youth being trained for such important national duties must accept the idea of following the Führer absolutely and without question, without damaging discontentment, criticism, without self-regard or resistance.

Religion: God and nation are the two foundations of the life of the individual and the community.

Although the German school system under the Nazis was designed to inhibit intellectual advancement and was geared to conditioning women to accept a submissive, secondary role in society, many of those who attended state schools during the Third Reich considered themselves to have been well educated.

The three-tier system of education that exists in Germany today was operating then. *Volksschule* catered for children from the ages of 7 until 11 and had segregated classes for boys and girls. At the end of the fourth year, pupils had the choice to stay on for another four years, after which they could leave full-time education without a qualification, or go on to a grammar school (high school) or a *Gymnasium* (comprehensive) for a further six years.

Both were exclusively for boys. If girls wanted to continue their education, their parents had to pay for them to attend a private school or *Lyceum*.

In secondary school, English was frequently taught as a

first foreign language with French as the second language. Boys might also be taught Latin. Grammar school girls would typically be taught secretarial skills, domestic science, needle-work, art and music in addition to the basic subjects.

History was literally rewritten to emphasize the positive aspects of German nationalism and to apportion blame for the defeat of 1918 to the convenient scapegoats – the vindic-tive Allied victors and the Jews.

The subject of racial purity pervaded practically every subject from biology to geography, with an emphasis on the need for *Lebensraum* [living space for the German people]. The preservation of the 'superior' Aryan bloodline was emphasized and illustrated with insidious propaganda films comparing the Jews to plague-spreading vermin. These were enforced with film and photographs of mentally and physi-cally disabled people to justify the state's policy of forced sterilization and euthanasia.

Fanciful racial theories were introduced to pupils from the age of six under the generic subject *Rassenkunde* [race know-ledge] and were presented as proven fact of the superiority of the Aryan master race and the inferiority of the Jews and Slavic races. Students had no opportunity to question the validity of these theories as all Jews had been excluded from the public school system after 1935 under the Nuremberg Laws.

Older students also studied Philosophical Propadeutic (the history of philosophy), which had been introduced to instruct them in the specious unfounded beliefs of Nazi 'philosopher' Alfred Rosenberg, whose anti-Semitic diatribe *The Myth of the Twentieth Century* was the set text for the course. Its central argument was that man lacks a soul but is guided by intuition. According to Rosenberg, 'great men' such as Hitler were able to inspire their followers by appealing to their intuition, in the same way as religious leaders were believed to be able to raise the consciousness of their devotees and disciples. Hitler was said to have dismissed the book as pure gibberish, but it remained on the syllabus because it was marginally more comprehensible than *Mein Kampf*. In contrast, almost every textbook was peppered with quotes from the latter. Even a fifth-grade biology book for girls equated the hierarchy of the animal kingdom with the German nation's superiority and right to subjugate 'inferior' races:

'He who wants to live must fight, and he who does not want to fight in this world of perpetual struggle does not deserve to live!'

(Adolf Hitler, *Mein Kampf*)

And on the same page, the future mothers of the nation were reminded of their Führer's assertion that:

'The world does not exist for cowardly nations!'

It was also explicitly stated that the purpose of education was to prepare girls for motherhood and boys for the military:

'The goal of female education must be to prepare them for motherhood.'

(*Mein Kampf*)

'The task of the army in the ethnic state is not to train the individual in marching, but to serve as the highest school for education in service of the Fatherland.'

(*Mein Kampf*)

Physical fitness became a core subject in the curriculum; attendance was compulsory and ruthless competitiveness was rewarded. Failure to attain a minimum standard of fitness could result in expulsion, while exceeding the required standard might bring the pupil to the attention of the selection board of the elite Adolf Hitler schools, which had been founded to identify suitable candidates for the SS.

> *'The weak must be chiselled away. I want young men and women who can suffer pain. A young German must be as swift as a greyhound, as tough as leather, and as hard as Krupp's steel.'*

Adolf Hitler

When the war began, there was a shortage of experienced teachers. This meant that two or more classes had to be combined. In the rural districts, classes were increased to 45 or more pupils per class to take children who had been evacuated from the cities.

Discipline was extremely strict and enforced with corporal punishment. Pupils were expected to stand to attention when a teacher entered and give the Hitler salute. There were no school uniforms, but every child was expected to wear their Hitler Youth or BDM uniform on special days such as Hitler's birthday (20 April 1889) and the anniversary of the Beer Hall Putsch (9 November 1923), when Hitler and the brown shirts had staged a failed uprising in Munich.

The innate mischievousness and distrust of authority of young adolescents could not be suppressed so easily, however. It was not unknown for otherwise conscientious pupils to distract a teacher from setting an exam by asking a question about Hitler or the origins of the party, knowing that this would set them off on a long discourse, leaving insufficient time for the test.

Outsiders

Life in Hitler's Germany was very different for non-Aryan children.

Ten-year-old Susan Oppenheimer considered herself happy and carefree until her teachers and school friends began to behave differently towards her in the spring of 1933. Non-Aryan children were moved to the back of the class and excluded from certain lessons, including PE, but never given an explanation. Susan had been particularly good at German, but she was told that her essays would no longer be read out to the class because 'only a true German could be good at German'. Fortunately, she was able to continue her athletics training by joining a club for the children of former First World War veterans, as her father had been in the German army during the Great War. But gradually her Aryan friends stopped talking to her and she was left with only Jewish children for company. Her former friends had joined the Hitler Youth and no longer spoke to her. If they did it was only to hurl abuse at her, which hurt Susan enormously. She couldn't understand why they hated her.

Then, in the summer of 1938, all non-Aryan pupils were prohibited from attending German state schools and Susan had to enrol at a private college. There, students were taught subjects that would be of use to them if they were forced to emigrate, as many were now expecting to do. But then came *Kristallnacht* and intimidation and discrimination took on a more violent and explicit form.

One of the first acts implemented by the new regime was the passing of a law which excluded Jews from government posts and the professions, forbade them from frequenting specific public places, such as parks, and from participating in public life and forcing them to identify themselves by wearing a yellow star on their clothes.

Susan remembered being woken that night by shouting and screaming as eight young storm troopers burst into the family home and began to vandalize everything in sight. They locked her parents in a bathroom, then attacked Susan and her younger sister. The girls were dragged out of bed and Susan's nightgown was ripped to shreds. Her parents could be heard shouting and crying but were unable to intervene. Then the SA thugs ordered Susan to get dressed, but as she opened the wardrobe they pulled it down on top of her and left, assuming they had killed her. Fortunately, it had fallen onto an overturned table, which left just enough room for the terrified teenager to crawl out and comfort her sister, who had shielded herself with blankets now covered with broken mirror glass.

The next day the family cleared up the wreckage of their apartment with the help of an elderly maid who admitted she was a staunch admirer of Hitler and who could not believe that he had sanctioned such wanton destruction.

Later that morning Susan took her bicycle to visit family friends to see if they were all right – no one dared use the phone for fear that it was being tapped by the Gestapo. All had suffered traumatic experiences the previous night. Now they urged each other to leave the city as the notorious Jew-baiter Julius Streicher was organizing a mass rally for that evening at which it was feared he would call for more attacks on the Jews of Nuremberg. The Oppenheimer family decided to drive to the British consulate in Munich but they were stopped soon after they reached the city, their father was arrested and the car confiscated. When their mother enquired when she might see her husband again she was told that they would be sent his ashes. As Susan later learned, her father was already on his way to Dachau.

Judy Benton had a similar experience as a schoolgirl in Meissen near Dresden. She too was moved to the back of the class, but had the added indignity of sitting at a desk painted yellow and inscribed: 'Here sits a dirty Jewish girl.' The teacher refused to mark her work and she was denied the first prize for coming top in her class, after being told that she had earned it. But she didn't complain when she was informed that the prize was a copy of *Mein Kampf*.

Judy remembered with some bitterness that the teachers rarely failed to find an opportunity to ridicule her. On one occasion a teacher brought in a poster purporting to explain how to identify a Jew: it listed black hair, a large hooked nose and yellowed fingers from counting money.

Judy's father had lost his business, a small factory producing household goods, after the Nazis seized it. One day she returned home from school to find the door open and her parents gone. A neighbour told her they had been taken by the Gestapo and she would be arrested if she remained. Showing great presence of mind, she took her passport, some money that her mother had hidden for emergencies and a small suitcase and joined a *Kindertransport* taking unaccompanied children to safety in Britain.

Without a guarantor to sponsor her and meet her at the other end of her journey, she was taking an enormous risk. But after she arrived at the station and was approached by weeping mothers begging her to look after their young children, she had the bright idea of buying a nurse's costume from a fancy-dress shop and posing as a nurse. It was an idea that saved her life.

American-born Frederic C. Tubach travelled in the opposite direction. In 1933, at the age of three, he was taken by his German parents from the safety of their home in San Francisco to Germany, where he met and befriended children of both Nazi and anti-Nazi families as well as several who were divided by their political beliefs.

His own father joined the party but his mother was adamantly opposed to extremists of any kind. He recalls that the Nazis shrewdly seduced every branch of society into believing that National Socialism would benefit all members of the community and made sure that they had a strong visual presence in every town. One particularly effective example was the large bright-red collection box for the poor, which fostered a feeling of solidarity within a community. Everyone, even those who didn't have much to spare themselves, contributed in the belief that they were helping their less fortunate neighbours.

For children, the big attraction was knowing they were getting 'Uncle Adolf's' approval if they excelled at sport. As an added incentive, outstanding performance in sport earned promotion in the Hitler Youth, so children began to be more aware of their grades and tried to exceed their previous best performance. Frederic remembers that he and his friends were encouraged in their love of sport by the cigarette companies that produced collectible cards of the German Olympic athletes who became their heroes.

Moulding Young Minds

'Our state ... does not let a man go free from the cradle to the grave. We start our work when the child is three. As soon as it begins to think a little flag is put into its hand. Then comes school, the Hitler Youth, the Storm Troopers and military training. We don't let a single soul go, and when all that is done, there is the Labour Front which takes possession of them when they are grown up and does not let them go until they die, whether they like it or not.'

(Dr Robert Ley, leader of the Nazi Labour Front)

When he was 13, Frederic was chosen to attend a Nazi development camp where he observed at first-hand how the Nazis moulded young minds. When the boys in his room were questioned about an incident that would have had them expelled from school, they refused to give up the guilty boy and were instead congratulated for showing solidarity. 'They weren't interested in morality or social behaviour,' he concluded. 'The message was "you can do what you want, you can let your teenage violent impulses out, it doesn't matter, as long as you do it for us".'

He found the Hitler Youth leaders unconvincing because what they taught was 'emotional and inconsistent'. The Nazis, in his opinion, were not as well practised in control techniques as the Stalinists, who exercised control over every aspect of daily life:

'The fact that Nazi concepts were so vague and unsupported by historical facts gave licence to the fanatics to say whatever moved them, as long as it stimulated hate and prejudice. Family was more important for most of us. If the family was anti-Nazi, odds were the child would be. That's a big reason the Nazis wanted to undermine the family.'

As a result of the Reich Labour Service Law, passed in June 1935, all young men between the ages of 18 and 25 were compelled to leave home and live in work camps for six months where they participated in communal programmes such as ditch-digging and marsh-draining. At the same time, their fathers might be attending party meetings, their mother engaged in the social activities organized by the League of German Girls and their younger siblings hiking with the Hitler Youth. Far from preserving the traditional German family, as it had promised to do, the regime was actively isolating the children from parental influence and working on each family member to ensure that their loyalty was primarily to the party. Parental influence was further undermined by the knowledge that their children had the power to inform on them, if only out of pique when there was a disagreement. Children were also encouraged to take an 'active interest' in the political opinions of their parents by their teachers, who would ask them to write essays on family life and the topics discussed by their parents.

The Church at that time exerted a strong moral influence on a sizeable proportion of the population, particularly in the predominantly Catholic south, specifically Bavaria. For this reason the Nazis actively sought to undermine the authority of the Church by imposing its own neo-pagan religion, with Nazi-themed weddings and funerals in which the Bible was replaced by *Mein Kampf*, the Holy Cross by the swastika and Christ was supplanted by Hitler.

However, religious conviction prevented many devout Christians from accepting Hitler as the new messiah. Nevertheless, young men such as Professor Tubach felt at the time that the mantra they chanted at each meeting of the *Jungvolk* in honour of the Führer was intended to invest Hitler with a special aura and empower his followers in the same way that a communal hymn gives the worshipper a sense of the divine.

Professor Tubach also recalled that in camp he and his young comrades were encouraged to make as much noise as they wished while they awaited meals and at meetings – in stark contrast to the customary prayer that many would have been expected to say at home. Evidently the party wanted to subvert the boys' traditional religious upbringing in order to destroy 'moral sensibilities and civilized behaviour'.

These asocial impulses were seen as positive attributes by the authors of the various leadership manuals:

'The protection of the home and bourgeois behaviour are despised. Industriousness in school is discarded for the sake of courage and physical prowess.'
(*Geist der Jungmannschaft*, 1934)

Hitler Youth

'In my Ordensburgen ... a youth will grow up that will horrify the world. I want to have a violent, lordly fearless, cruel youth ... They have to suffer and conquer pain. Nothing gentle and weak in them must be left.'
(Hitler, *Der Nationalsozialismus. Dokumente 1939–1945*, ed. Walther Hofer)

One of the many crimes committed by the Nazi leadership for which they were not indicted at Nuremberg was the betrayal of the nation's youth. During the 12 years of Nazi rule, a generation of young people were indoctrinated with the regime's specious racial ideology, conditioned to submit to authority without question and compelled to join youth organizations that suppressed their individuality in order to create soulless, obedient automatons.

Ilse McKee was 11 years old when Hitler came to power in 1933, the year membership of the Hitler Youth increased rapidly from 50,000 to more than two million. The organization

The Hitler Youth was conceived as a precursor to military service and emphasized strict discipline, order and unquestioning loyalty and obedience to the leadership.

had been formed in 1926, but regular attendance is believed to have been as low as 25 per cent until membership became compulsory in December 1936, when its ranks swelled to more than four million (90 per cent of the nation's youth).

It has been generally accepted that membership of the Nazi youth groups was compulsory, with every Aryan boy over the age of 14 obliged to join the Hitler Youth and those between 10 and 14 required to enrol in the *Jungvolk*, but it was not mandatory until 1939.

Without doubt the most popular activities for boys were the *Geländespiele* [war games], which required stealth, strategy and surprise to outmanoeuvre and capture a pre-arranged landmark from the defending team. But even this innocent children's game was adapted to encourage self-sacrifice for the common good, rather than encouraging a rational solution that achieved its objective with the minimum loss of life. It was obvious to even the most subservient, unthinking member of the Hitler Youth that their training had little to do with scouting and more to do with soldiering.

Girls were required to join the League of German Girls and its sister organization, the Young Girls, bringing total membership of the four youth groups to seven and a half million, or three-quarters of those eligible to join. But many young people had been inducted after their non-political youth organization had been dissolved and their members were automatically enrolled in the Nazi Youth groups. Even then, there were ways to avoid attendance on medical grounds or simply by virtue of having to study, which left no time for extracurricular activities.

The two female branches of the *Bund Deutscher Mädel* [BDM, League of German Girls] initially proved more popular than the equivalent male organizations because they offered girls the opportunity to participate in activities that had been considered more suitable for boys, such as hiking. In addition, they promised to teach them subjects that were not included on the state school curriculum, namely arts, crafts, music and theatre as well as the making and mending of their own clothes and basic domestic skills.

Not everyone in the Nazi leadership, however, was impressed by their newfound skills and discipline. Himmler was overheard to remark that when he saw girls marching in ranks dressed in their brown *Kletterjacke* [climbing jackets], white blouse and dark blue skirts, he felt sick to his stomach. Parents, too, had their reservations, particularly those who

Hitler declared that the National Socialist revolution would be an entirely male event and was horrified to see women marching in uniform at the Nuremberg Rallies.

would have preferred to see their children in church on a
Sunday morning rather than going on group outings.

Girls between the ages of 10 and 14 were encouraged to join
the *Jungmädel* [Young Girls' League], the junior branch of the
BDM, whose only qualifications for entry were proof of
racial purity and a minimum standard of fitness and athletic
ability. Girls were required to attend twice-weekly evening
classes and to be present at every youth rally and sports
event. Weekends were a continuous programme of group
activities involving hiking with a full pack, scavenger hunts,
camping and fund-raising events. These activities proved
beneficial for physical fitness, but left the girls little time for
their school work. Consequently, many failed to acquire a
basic education or obtain essential qualifications. It was
common for teachers to complain that pupils were too tired
to stay awake in class the morning after attending an
evening BDM meeting.

Evening classes were invariably taken by girls not much
older than those they were instructing and consisted mainly
of songs and political lectures, which the older girls taught by
rote, often with little understanding of what they were
teaching. In order to maintain discipline, drills would be
organized during which the girls were marched up and down
like soldiers on a parade ground while the *Scharfuehrerinnen*
[group leaders] barked orders. It must have seemed pointless
to girls of that age, especially when they were being
constantly told that they were being prepared for
motherhood.

Both the boys' and girls' classes would be held in the same
building so that they could all attend the lectures on racial
topics and the importance of raising the birth rate. Ilse

McKee recalls being unable to suppress a giggle at the thought of the 'spidery-legged, pimply little cockerels' who were expected to father the soldiers of the future. Inevitably, there were numerous unplanned teenage pregnancies, of which the boys boasted and about which the girls felt a sense of pride rather than shame, as they considered it their duty to breed babies like battery hens.

Ballot Rigging

Once the Nazis were in power they could take it for granted that the result in any future elections or plebiscites (referendums) would be in their favour. Unfortunately for them, in the March 1936 election their ballot rigging caused them some embarrassment when the result gave them exactly 99 per cent of the votes in every district of Berlin. In Friedrichshagen, 15 voting centres recorded as many votes as there were registered voters and the remaining five centres had only one vote less. As *Gauleiter* [party leader] of Berlin, Dr Goebbels was not amused and ordered a meeting of local party officials and activists at which he warned them to be more circumspect in future.

In Hamburg, ballot papers for the national plebiscite on Germany's reoccupation of the Rhineland had been numbered in invisible ink and those who voted against were subsequently arrested. Knowing this, trainee lawyer Peter Bielenberg volunteered to assist with the count in his district of Berlin later that same year – in a vote called to approve more of the party's policies – and was elated to see that many had voted 'no'. But the next morning the newspapers declared a unanimous vote in the party's favour, confirming what every free-thinking German had feared: the opposition had been effectively silenced and more severe measures would need to be taken to remove the dictator.

Chapter Three
Myth of the Master Race

Getting in Step

'It don't mean a thing if it ain't got that swing.'
(Duke Ellington)

While all of Germany seemed to be marching in step behind their leader, there was a small but significant number of non-conformists who chose to dance to a different tune. Although it took considerable courage to openly flout the diktats of a totalitarian regime, the 'swing kids', as they became known, were not particularly politically astute, nor were they all ideologically opposed to the Nazis on principle. Many were simply adolescents who were determined to exercise their right to do as they damn well pleased. They resented being told what they were allowed to wear, how to cut their hair and what music they were forbidden to listen to. The fact that they were living under the most repressive regime in modern times did not deter them from asserting their individuality and cocking a snoot at authority.

In the mid-1930s, a new form of up-tempo American jazz with a syncopated rhythm was electrifying the airwaves all around the world and filling ballroom and nightclub dance floors with jitterbugging teens. They called it swing and German youth saw no reason why they should be forced to sit on the sidelines and watch the free world have their fun. The regime had made it known that they disapproved of this lascivious 'jungle music' and its flamboyant fashions, which they denounced as ostentatious and decadent. Both were said to be part of a global conspiracy to undermine National Socialism and contaminate Aryan culture.

The music was condemned for encouraging casual sex, excessive drinking and intimate interracial relationships. So the swing fans went underground, partying in private houses and in the basements of bars and cafés while continuing to flaunt their defiance in public with their flashy dress sense and hairstyles favoured by American movie stars and the reputedly dissolute English upper class.

Boys backcombed their long hair with brilliantine as if to show their contempt for the military short-back-and-sides that was mandatory in the Hitler Youth, while the girls adopted long, coiffured hairstyles in contrast to the traditional braids worn by the female members of the BDM.

The swing kids tended to come from the middle and upper classes of German society because the clothes and accessories were comparatively expensive and the lifestyle could be maintained only by the more affluent offspring.

There were regional variations, but boys generally identified themselves by dressing in knee-length zoot suits with baggy double-breasted jackets that had wide lapels, which they had seen in photographs of American jazz musicians, with perhaps a trench coat as worn by the tough guys of American gangster films, such as Humphrey Bogart and

James Cagney. Trouser turn-ups were obligatory, as were crepe-soled shoes and a pipe or a folded foreign newspaper to signal where one's allegiance lay. A Homburg with a 'gutter crown' and 'kettle-curl' brim or a wide-brimmed fedora completed the image.

Girls copied the Hollywood fashion icons as far as the restrictions on imported clothes, shoes and cosmetics allowed. The use of make-up was frowned upon by the Nazis, who viewed it as a sign of sexual promiscuity and declared it to be contrary to the natural healthy appearance of the Aryan female, so the girls applied as much as they could and in as many garish colours as they could find. It was common knowledge that the wives of Nazi officials continued to wear lipstick, nail polish, mascara and face powder in Hitler's presence and their swing sisters didn't see why they too should be denied the opportunity to look attractive.

In open defiance of Hitler's abhorrence of French haute couture and masculine attire, the swing 'chicks' mimicked the slim, boyish, pinched-waist style made popular by Parisian models and the trouser suits that movie icons Katharine Hepburn and Bette Davis had made an essential part of their image. The Hollywood stars provided the swing girls with elegant, confident role models and were often filmed or photographed affecting a carefree pose while drawing on a long cigarette holder, which the German girls also copied in defiance of Hitler's known distaste for smoking, particularly in women.

It was not only the clothes that defined a hepcat and a hip chick, but also the street slang they used, as well as their cool, laid-back attitude and swagger – the antithesis of the strict discipline instilled into the stiff-necked Hitler Youth.

Female swing kids mimicked the fashions set by Hollywood movie icons and played with sexual stereotypes to provoke their elders and the Nazi establishment.

But the swing kids were more than a rebellious youth movement or provocative fashion statement. They were passionate fans of the music that symbolized personal freedom. The fact that it was effectively banned in Germany meant that simply listening to it on the BBC or on American overseas broadcasts was to risk arrest. But prohibition made it all the more appealing.

As records were hard to obtain and gramophones were a rarity, some swing fans made illegal copies for themselves and friends using small portable disc cutters, which put them at even greater risk. However, the majority heard their jazz in the clubs and at private parties, which were organized by someone who owned or had managed to borrow a gramophone.

For some, it was not enough just to listen or dance. They wanted to play the music themselves and soon home-grown swing bands were playing in the style of Duke Ellington, Woody Herman, Benny Goodman and Count Basie. Goebbels attempted to counter the craze by forming the regime's own rival to Basie, the innocuously named Charlie and his Orchestra, who performed pro-Nazi numbers for foreign propaganda broadcasts, but their music was as phoney as Hitler's promises.

Although there was never the possibility that a love of jazz might form the foundation for a real resistance movement, the authorities were alarmed to learn that the free form dance routines included overtly provocative gestures, such as a version of the Hitler salute incorporating Churchill's 'V' for Victory sign. Mocking the *Sieg Heil* salute was prohibited by law, so doing so even behind closed doors was a violation punishable by imprisonment. And being under the age of legal responsibility was no defence. In October 1942, 17-year-old Helmuth Hübener became the youngest of 16,500 people to be beheaded by guillotine during the Hitler years. His crime was distributing anti-war leaflets based on BBC broadcasts.

But the threat of such grim retribution did not appear to dampen the enthusiasm of the swing kids. Other seemingly innocent phrases in English or Yiddish were sprinkled into casual conversation to identify a fellow swing fan ('Swing Heil' being the most common greeting or parting phrase) or to provoke outrage from eavesdroppers and passers-by.

In 1940, the authorities attempted to crack down on the movement by installing a curfew on under-18s, but it proved almost impossible to enforce as the swing kids routinely used counterfeit identity papers to gain entrance to the clubs, bars and dance halls. Even without such papers, it was difficult to determine their true age due to their adult attire and the girls' heavy use of make-up.

The craze was so endemic in certain cities that an official report was commissioned by the Reich Ministry of Justice in spring 1944 that concluded:

'These cliques begin their activities out of a selfish impulse to amuse themselves, but rapidly deteriorate into antisocial criminal gangs. Even before the war, boys and girls from the elite social set in Hamburg would get together dressed in notorious baggy or loose clothing and become entranced under the spell of English music and dance. They often wear jackets cut in the Scot slit manner, carry umbrellas, and put fancy-coloured collar-studs in their jacket lapels as badges of their arrogance. They mimic the decadent English way of life, because they worship the Englishman as the highest evolutionary development of mankind.'

The Flottbecker Clique in Hamburg was singled out for censure by the Justice Ministry for organizing 'lewd affairs' at which up to 600 teenagers had indulged in 'unrestrained swing dancing' during the winter of 1939–40 and for openly opposing the Hitler Youth by refusing to conform and join the movement. But even after the authorities had imposed a ban on these private parties, the defiant teens continued to organize 'unlawful jamborees full of sexual mischief'.

By war's end the authorities were confident that 'evacuation methods necessitated by wartime conditions' had helped to break up these groups.

A Mixed Blessing

The swing kids were an exclusively white, middle- and upper-class clique who shared a passion for hot 'exotic' American jazz and its milder English variation. But there was one young man among them for whom the music was more than a mere adolescent obsession. Hans-Jürgen Massaquoi was a talented saxophonist whose musicianship would save himself and his mother from starvation after the war when he found employment playing for American merchant seamen in Hamburg clubs. But during the Hitler years, Massaquoi had the unique experience of being one of the few black German children growing up in the Third Reich.

As the son of mixed-race parents (his absent father was a West African law student and his mother a white German national), he was excluded but not persecuted by the regime, although he suffered racist abuse at school and at the hands of other children in his neighbourhood. He believed that he escaped deportation or worse simply because the regime didn't feel there were enough mixed-race children to necessitate a round-up.

Massaquoi was brought up by his mother to believe that he was a German 'just like everybody else' and so he couldn't understand why his teachers refused to allow him to join the Hitler Youth. He wanted to enrol so he could participate in all the activities his friends were enjoying and he admired their smart uniform.

'The Nazis put on the best show of all the political parties. There were parades, fireworks and uniforms – these were the devices by which Hitler won over young people to his ideas.'

So after nagging his mother he was allowed to enlist in a branch called the *Deutsches Jungvolk*, which brought suspicious looks from the other blond, blue-eyed Aryan boys. But Massaquoi refused to be intimidated.

As the grandson of a wealthy Liberian consul official, he enjoyed a privileged childhood in a villa on the Johnsallee and was surrounded by white servants, which led him to believe that being black meant that he belonged to the superior class. But after his father and grandfather returned to Liberia in 1929, when the boy was just three years old, his mother was forced to find work as a poorly paid hospital assistant, which barely covered the rent on their tiny new flat in a working-class district of Hamburg.

But he recovered some of his injured pride after being taken on a school trip to the Olympic Games in Berlin in 1936, where he witnessed black athlete Jesse Owens beat the supposedly superior Aryan athletes. Also that summer, American boxer Joe Louis, the 'Brown Bomber', KO'd Hitler's champion Max Schmeling in the first round of a return bout. After this, Massaquoi's classmates nicknamed him 'Joe'.

As a second-class citizen he was later excused from military service, excluded from further education and prohibited from all professions, so he swallowed his pride and took a job as an apprentice machinist. After surviving the Allied bombing that reduced most of Hamburg to rubble in July 1943, he emigrated to the USA where he took a degree in journalism that eventually led to the editorship of *Ebony* magazine.

The Berlin Olympics

'I have now seen the famous German Leader and also something of the great change he has effected ... The old trust him. The young idolize him ... not a word of criticism or of disapproval have I heard of Hitler.'

(Former British Prime Minister David Lloyd George from 'I Talked To Hitler', *Daily Express*, 17 November 1936)

Hitler regarded the 1936 Berlin Olympics as an opportunity to promote National Socialism and prove the superiority of Aryan athletes. None of the 52 competing nations answered the call for a boycott and many teams lowered their flags in honour of the Führer as they marched passed the podium.

When Germany was given the honour of hosting the 1936 Olympic Games it was a cause for celebration throughout the country and a boost to national pride. In the eyes of its detractors, however, it served to legitimize the National Socialist revolution that was enforcing its iron rule with medieval barbarity, including torture, punishment beatings and beheadings.

Now the world's press would be invited to marvel at the changes that had taken place in the capital of the Reich and its critics would have to eat their words. That was the hope of Joseph Goebbels, who saw the games as an opportunity for the regime to showcase the remarkable achievements of National Socialism. He commented, 'Think of the press as a great keyboard on which the government can play.'

Hitler was not enthusiastic at first, but he understood the importance of the event in promoting sport among the nation's youth and also the opportunity that the games provided for the regime to prove Aryan superiority in athletics.

The Nazi leadership was so sure of success that it commissioned film-maker Leni Riefenstahl to record the event for propaganda purposes and posterity. Although her male colleagues in the industry pulled every stunt to sabotage her efforts, Hitler's backing ensured she was eventually given all the resources she required to make one of the most impressive and politically questionable documentaries ever made. In a particularly effective sequence, Riefenstahl depicted her sportsmen and women as living statues to represent the Aryan ideal of physical strength and beauty and to draw a comparison with the athletes of ancient Greece.

The decision to stage the games in Berlin had actually been made a year before the Nazis came to power, but this was brushed aside by the Propaganda Ministry at the press conference announcing the news, as were questions regarding the circumstances under which the International Olympic Committee (IOC) had reluctantly agreed to stage the 11th Olympiad in the heart of Hitler's Reich. Members of the committee had expressed alarm at reports in the foreign press of the imprisonment of political opponents and the persecution of minorities, specifically the exclusion of Jewish athletes who were well known in the athletics community. In fact, some members of the IOC were so concerned that they should not be seen to condone the regime's iniquitous racial laws that they argued bitterly among themselves and lobbied for a vote to withdraw the offer and stage the event elsewhere. The Nazi leadership was equally adamant that Germany should not be denied its propaganda coup and ordered German committee member Dr Karl Ritter von Halt to write to the IOC president denying the rumours and reports:

'Events in Germany are solely to do with domestic policies. In individual cases sportsmen have been affected. If a certain anti-German press feels called upon to deliver these domestic German matters on to the Olympic stage, then this is extraordinarily regrettable and shows their unfriendliness towards Germany in the worst possible light.'

The Reich minster for sport, Hans von Tschammer und Osten, made no apology for his country's overtly racist policies:

'We shall see to it that in our national life and in our relations and competitions with other nations, only such Germans shall be allowed to represent the nation as those against whom no objection can be raised.'

As a consequence of such statements, a number of American athletes who had qualified for the games chose to boycott the event, but they were not in sufficient numbers to make an impact.

Had America and other Western democracies taken a firm stand against fascism by withdrawing en masse from the games, it is arguable that the Nazis might have been forced to curb their programme of persecution and perhaps even reconsider their subsequent territorial demands.

Not even the German reoccupation of the Rhineland in March, nor the outbreak of the Spanish Civil War in July (which put paid to a rival event planned for Barcelona) deterred the IOC from organizing what German diarist Victor Klemperer called 'an entirely political enterprise'. And to ensure the success of that enterprise, Klemperer observed:

'The chanted slogans on the streets have been banned (for the duration of the Olympiad), Jew-baiting, bellicose sentiments, everything offensive has disappeared from the papers until the 16th of August ... In articles written in English the attention of "our guests" is repeatedly drawn to how peaceably and pleasantly things are proceeding here ... we have everything in abundance. But the butcher here and the greengrocer complain about shortages and price rises because everything has to be sent to Berlin.'

The diarist noted that the 'most loathsome' aspect of the Nazis' campaign to win hearts and minds abroad is that the state pretends to be 'an open book', but 'who chose and prepared the passages at which the book lies open? The dictatorship carries out its oppression in secret and acts hypocritically in the extreme while publicly condemning the

French Popular Front for its support of the Spanish communists. The Nazis protest, "We are not conducting a crusade. We do not shed blood either, we are a completely peaceable people and only want to be left in peace!" And at the same time not the smallest opportunity for propaganda is missed.'

The regime had learned from its mistakes in staging the Winter Olympics in February that year, when the foreign press reported seeing military manoeuvres at the site in Garmisch-Partenkirchen in the Bavarian Alps and had published photographs of anti-Jewish signs that were prominently displayed in public places. The locals had taken it upon themselves to erect these notices and had passed a bylaw prohibiting the conduct of business in Hebrew, as well as prohibiting Jews from buying or renting property in the town. Nine months before the games were scheduled to begin, the head of the organizing committee, Karl Ritter von Halt, a member of the SA, had written to the Interior Ministry to express his concerns regarding the groundswell of anti-Semitism in the area. 'I am not expressing my concerns in order to help the Jews,' he assured the Ministry, 'but if the propaganda is continued in this form the population of Garmisch-Partenkirchen will be so inflamed that it will indiscriminately attack and injure anyone who even looks Jewish.'

For the summer games, all signs banning Jews were removed, anti-Semitic posters were taken down, the military presence in the capital was reduced and 800 gypsies were rounded up and interned in a suburb of the city out of sight of the tourists. In addition, the police were instructed to disregard any minor infringements of the state's oppressive anti-homosexual laws for the duration and to keep a low profile. Behind the scenes, though, the regime refused to relax its stranglehold on censorship.

The Reich Press Chamber under Goebbels issued numerous edicts in advance of the opening ceremony to ensure that German journalists knew where their loyalties lay and what was expected from them.

They were warned not to mention that there were two non-Aryans in the women's national team or the possibility that one of them might win a gold medal in case she failed to do so.

The black athletes were not to be referred to in racial terms in case this offended the Americans and, above all, if they printed anything prior to the publication of the official and state-approved press report, they would be doing so at their own risk.

And so the 11th Olympiad of modern times opened with much pomp and pageantry on 1 August 1936, witnessed by a capacity crowd of 100,000, including ambassadors, envoys and invited guests. Among them was the aviator Charles Lindbergh, who had been rewarded for his public expressions of admiration for the New Order.

The *Hindenburg* airship flew overhead trailing the Olympic flag to an enthusiastic roar from the crowd, followed by a fanfare of trumpets as Hitler entered flanked by the officials from the Olympic Committee in their frock coats and top hats. As a military band struck up a march by Richard Strauss, the entire crowd seemed to rise to their feet en masse, raising their arms in the Hitler salute and yelling, 'Sieg Heil!'

To the evident delight of Goebbels and the other Nazi dignitaries, none of the 52 competing nations had answered the call for a boycott and the majority of the visiting teams marched past the dais lowering their flags in honour of their host and giving the fascist salute. Only the

The gold (Jesse Owens), silver (Luz Long) and bronze (Naoto Tajima) medal winners of the long jump competition salute from the victory podium at the 1936 Olympic Games, held in Berlin. The Games were the first in Olympic history to be broadcast live.

Americans held their banners aloft, which drew derisive whistles from the crowd. Later the Nazis explained the slight as due to official US army regulations that forbade the team from lowering the flag for anyone other than the American president.

Goebbels declared the day 'A victory for the German cause', despite the fact that black American athlete Jesse Owens had made a mockery of Aryan supremacy in full view of the world's press. One of two Jewish American sprinters later claimed that they were substituted by Owens and another runner the day before the 4 x 100-metre relay in order to spare Hitler the sight of two Jews on the winning podium. This was denied by the coach who explained that he simply wanted to go with his two fastest sprinters.

The New York Times concluded:

> '*For [Hitler] it has been a day of triumph, exceeding perhaps any that have gone before. From soon after dawn, when a military parade down Unter den Linden and back revived the old imperial custom of "Great Waiting", until he retired past midnight, he was the object of enthusiasm exceeding all bounds. These Olympic Games have had an opening notable even beyond expectations, high as these were. They seem likely to accomplish what the rulers of Germany have frankly desired from them, that is, to give the world a new viewpoint from which to regard the Third Reich: it is promising that this viewpoint will be taken from an Olympic hill of peace.*'

But not every journalist who went to Berlin was seduced by the obsequious smiles and the insincere hospitality. One British newspaper described the summer games as 'a Nazi party rally disguised as a sporting event', while Berlin correspondent William S. Shirer wrote scathingly in his diary on 16 August:

> '*I'm afraid the Nazis have succeeded with their propaganda. First, the Nazis have run the Games on a lavish scale never before experienced, and this has appealed to the athletes. Second, the Nazis have put up a very good front for the general visitors, especially the businessmen.*'

Despite Hitler's refusal to acknowledge Jesse Owens' crowd-pleasing performance in public or the achievement of 13

Jewish medal-winning athletes (including a silver for German fencer Helene Mayer and a bronze for Austria's Ellen Preis), the Führer considered the event to have been a triumph. He told his architect Albert Speer that henceforth every Olympiad would take place in Berlin. (The next Olympic Games were scheduled to be staged in Tokyo in 1940, which the outbreak of war made impossible.)

Behind the scenes, however, the Berlin Olympics proved to be something of a curse for several of those who participated.

Two days after the closing ceremony, the head of the Olympic Village, Captain Wolfgang Fürstner, committed suicide after being dismissed from the army on account of his Jewish ancestry. The following year, after being denied a place in the German team, high-jump champion Gretel Bergmann fled Germany to escape the fate that befell so many of her fellow Jews. Had she been allowed to compete, it is believed she could have won another gold for her country.

But it is Owens whom history remembers as the man who defied a dictator and revealed the fallacy of Aryan superiority. He was only one of 18 African-American athletes to take part in the Berlin Olympics, however, 14 of whom won a quarter of the 56 medals awarded to the United States. Ironically, all returned home to face segregation and prejudice in their own country. Owens earned nothing as an amateur athlete and was reduced to making what can only be described as degrading personal appearances in order to secure a living.

In the last weeks of the war the stadium was used by the SS to execute 200 'traitors', many of them in their teens. After Berlin had been reduced to rubble in 1945 it remained unscathed, a monument to a time when the world allowed itself to be seduced by a regime well practised in the art of deception.

Chapter Four
Living with the Enemy

Anschluss

Austrian Kitty Werthmann was 12 years old when her country voted overwhelmingly in favour of assimilation into the Reich in the March 1938 plebiscite. For Hitler, the former Austrian corporal who claimed to have starved as a penniless artist in Vienna in the years prior to the First World War, it was a personal triumph to return to the country of his birth and be fêted as its leader.

But Kitty could not understand why a 'Christian nation' had elected such a man.

In the late 1930s, Austria was suffering from high unemployment and rampant inflation and any politician who promised to sort it out would not have been scrutinized too closely. She recalled:

'Farmers were going broke, the banks had reclaimed their farms. In the business world, they were closing up one by one. They couldn't afford to pay interest. It wasn't unusual in my home to have about 30 people a day knocking on the door asking for a bowl of soup and a slice of bread. My

*own father was hanging on by a thread. The economy was
so bad, we could almost not exist.'*

If Germany had recovered from the Depression, then it
seemed reasonable to assume that Hitler would perform the
same economic miracle for his homeland. Kitty continues:

*'He didn't talk like a monster, he talked like an American
politician. We didn't hear anything bad, about him arresting
people and persecuting people. We thought he was a
great leader.'*

On the day Hitler drove through the streets of Vienna to a
hero's welcome from adoring crowds, there was an outbreak
of Jew-baiting that made some of the leading Nazis blanch.
But it was only later that it became evident that Hitler had
returned not as a prodigal son but as a conqueror:

*'We got free radios, then he nationalized the radio stations.
We were told if we listened to foreign broadcasting we were
an enemy of the state. Then he nationalized the banks, after
he looted all the Jewish banks.'*

After the war, the Austrians would talk ruefully of the Hitler
years as if they had been occupied by an invading force and
refer to the surrender as the 'armistice', but there are those
who see no distinction between Austrians and their Nazi
brethren.

Polish peasant Stefan Terlezki was 14 years old when he
was taken from his school by the Wehrmacht in 1942 and
transported in a cattle truck to Voitsberg near Graz. There he
was sold into slavery and worked almost to death by his

Austrian owner, a farmer. He survived by scavenging potatoes, which were so plentiful that no one noticed when one
or two went missing.

> '*Working on a farm was hell for the simple reason that as
> a slave you had no right to anything. You were just told,
> "do this, do that, come here, go there". In fact they never
> called me by my name, and I wondered whether I would
> ever be called Stefan, let alone anything else. I was called
> many things but not Stefan, and that was hard to swallow.
> Just imagine: 14 years of age and taken away into slavery.
> I had to look after myself. I had no shoulders to cry on,
> only my own.*'

Several hundred thousand people crowded into the Heldenplatz in
Vienna to hear Hitler's address from the balcony of the Hofburg, at
the time of the *Anschluss* [annexation], March 1938.

Preaching the Gospel

In the years immediately preceding the Nazi's accession to power, Hamburg housewife Christabel Bielenberg, who was British by birth, frequently found herself being lectured on the benefits of National Socialism by family friends and neighbours, whose intensity and dogged devotion to Hitler she found mildly amusing at first. She had become a German citizen on 29 September 1934, the same day she had married a young legal student, Peter Bielenberg, who would be imprisoned for his part in the failed July plot to kill Hitler ten years later. He would survive.

Christabel suspected that the young men she met who preached the Nazi creed hoped they might be able to convert her to their cause. But she had listened only out of politeness and curiosity. Her husband was ideologically opposed to fascism in any form and never tired of reminding her that the one time he had heard Hitler speak was in Hamburg Zoo.

Having lived in various lodgings in both the well-to-do and more modest districts of Hamburg during her student days, Christabel was familiar with the widely shared opinion on who was to blame for Germany's problems. From both the university professor that she had lodged with and the middle-class families with whom she later stayed, she heard the same arguments: the Prussian officer class had not lost the Great War, they had been 'stabbed in the back', by the Jews and the communists.

The Germans believed themselves to be the only nation that had suffered privations as a result of the war. Only Hitler understood their grievances and could bring stability and security to Germany, in the Reichstag and on the streets. He would end the violence by crushing the communists and he had promised to restore national pride by tearing up the hated Versailles Treaty and reclaiming the occupied territories taken from them after 1918. It was clear, even to a non-politically minded person such as Christabel, that this was an emotive issue and not one open to rational and reasoned debate. She found it wearisome to be harangued at every opportunity and was bemused by the ease and earnest sincerity with which they had swallowed Nazi propaganda as well as by their gushing devotion to Hitler. How could honest, hard-working Germans ever hope to get a decent job if they didn't have influential Jewish friends, they asked her. Many respectable German families had lost almost everything during the Depression. Only the Jews had thrived, she was told. Moreover, they had the facts and figures to prove it.

When Hitler became chancellor on 30 January 1933, she was pleased that these earnest people would now have the chance to see what their beloved Führer might do for Germany – she was quietly confident that they would soon be disillusioned and that another faction would be in power before too long.

But within two years the unmistakeable signs of a new dictatorship were visible in every town. Swastika flags fluttered from every public building, and main squares across the country had been renamed in honour of the Führer. The happy hikers she had once seen walking the country roads were now dressed in the uniforms of the Hitler Youth. The boys had had their hair cut short, the girls had woven theirs into plaits and many older men who had previously shown little interest in politics now sported a Hitler moustache. Individualism seemed to have evaporated overnight.

Christabel's husband found himself confronted by new requirements barring his way to his chosen profession that had nothing to do with academic ability or qualifications. All candidates had to prove their 'political reliability' and were required to submit to two months of intense political indoctrination at a semi-military camp, which would also put them through a strict physical regime.

However, for all the wariness that Christabel and Peter felt on witnessing the birth of the New Germany, it was difficult to deny that the atmosphere had changed for the better. Fear of a second financial crisis appeared to have been replaced by cautious optimism and a sense of purpose. Idle, unemployed youths who had previously loitered on street corners were now marching in smart uniforms, revealing a pride in their appearance and a gleam in their eye. Their elders were working with renewed vigour, confident that their efforts would be rewarded.

Although some had expressed disapproval of the methods Hitler had employed to purge the party of the rowdier element, it was generally accepted that the elimination of Roehm and his brown shirts on the 'Night of the Long Knives' in July 1934 had been necessary to restore order. The rivalry between the army and the SA that had threatened to erupt in a counter-revolution had been resolved and now the army was fully behind Hitler. Such unpleasantness was the price that had to be paid for the 'revolution', but now there was no more talk of dissent or pitched battles in the streets between rival political groups. And Hitler's merciless suppression of unruly elements within the SA had earned the grudging respect of the international community. Germany had regained its dignity and standing on the world stage. And everyone was once again proud to be a citizen of the Reich.

Christabel noticed that people seemed more cheerful and behaved more politely in public than before. They had regained their sense of self-worth and respectability and in return they were not inclined to question the leadership's methods. National Socialism was not so much a political programme as a secular cult that offered every loyal citizen what they had previously been deprived of – self-respect. Everyone, it seemed, had their place in the New Order and all were assured that their contribution was valued.

There was the promise of work for the unemployed, equal opportunities for everyone once the Jews had been legally excluded from the universities and professions, a level playing field for small businesses once the Jews had been forced out of theirs, long-term contracts for industry, a fully conscripted Armed Forces for the High Command, vital tasks for civil servants, prestigious titles for the bureaucrats and a new racially themed curriculum guaranteeing employment for the teachers. Even the ordinary housewife found her unpaid efforts in maintaining the home acknowledged and there were medals for mothers who bore the most children.

And for those lowly individuals without official status who desired to be known and to exercise power over their neighbours, there was the opportunity to be employed as block wardens of their apartment buildings and to play the intimidating role of informer.

In Berlin-Dahlem, Christabel was confronted with the fact that Herr Neisse, her gardener, now had the power to have her and her neighbours arrested on the merest suspicion of disloyalty. A careless remark or a failure to contribute generously to party collections could have fearful consequences.

Herr Neisse was typical of the 'common people' who had put their faith in Adolf Hitler after losing what little savings

Visitors to Nazi Germany were left in no doubt that they were in a totalitarian state.

they had in the Depression. They identified with the Führer with whom they shared humble origins and modest aspirations. And they had no reason to doubt him when he identified the cause of their plight and guaranteed to make sure they had work and food for their families, if they put their trust in the party and their mark in the appropriate box on their ballot papers.

Just like Corporal Hitler, Herr Neisse had fought in the Great War and he had worked hard on his return, saving up his marks and pfennigs for ten long years so that he would have enough to marry his sweetheart. He could not understand how some had profited from the hyperinflation of 1923, brought about when Germany defaulted on a reparations payment, while he had had his life savings wiped out and been reduced to living in poverty.

He had no particular dislike of Jews but he had come to resent what the Führer had called 'international Jewry', a mythical cabal of anonymous individuals who were apparently to blame for all of Germany's ills. Whether he truly believed in this convenient scapegoat or not, it served to explain what he didn't have the education or experience to understand. Besides, Herr Hitler was so convincing it would be ungrateful to doubt him. The Führer was devoted to Germany and he must have a good heart as he was routinely photographed with small children and dogs. Who could doubt his sincerity?

But true believers, such as Herr Neisse, were stumped when asked why the Führer had signed a non-aggression pact with the Bolsheviks, who only a week before had been caricatured on party postcards wielding vicious whips over defenceless German women and children. The Führer must know what he was doing and it was not for the likes of his followers to question the leader's reasons, was the response. In the meantime, the postcards had been withdrawn only to be replaced with identical images bearing a new caption. Instead of 'Conditions in Russian concentration camps', they now carried the caption 'British concentration camps in South Africa during the Boer War'.

The fact that the conditions in British internment camps bore no relation to the vicious cruelty meted out to the starved and brutalized victims interned in Nazi concentration camps did not occur to the likes of trusting, simple folk like Herr Neisse. As for the rumours that the party elite lived in luxury in their Berlin villas and merely paid lip service to National Socialism, Herr Neisse would say only that Hitler had no knowledge of such things. It was his answer to anything that sounded remotely critical of the regime. It didn't pay to tease Herr Neisse or press him on the subject or one might find oneself in his next report.

No one was to be trusted. Even the most casual conversation with a neighbour had to be guarded and free from any comment that might be misconstrued as expressing dissatisfaction with one's lot. One could never be sure that a chance encounter had not been engineered to catch one off guard and elicit some remark that could be used to prove disloyalty to the regime.

Living under Tyranny

'Most Germans, so far as I could see, did not seem to mind that their personal freedom had been taken away, that so much of their splendid culture was being destroyed and replaced with a mindless barbarism, or that their life and

*work were being regimented to a degree never before
experienced even by a people accustomed for generations to
a great deal of regimentation ... On the whole, people did
not seem to feel that they were being cowed and held down
by an unscrupulous tyranny. On the contrary, they appeared
to support it with genuine enthusiasm.'*

(William L. Shirer, *The Nightmare Years*)

Daily life for the ordinary citizen was overshadowed by the
ever-vigilant eye of the *Kreisleiter* or block wardens who
monitored and reported any infractions to the Gestapo. Some
80 per cent of Gestapo investigations were attributed to
informers (see: Roger Moorhouse, *Berlin at War*). Germans
were, in the main, respectful of authority and adhered to
rules and regulations. They prided themselves on
Ordungsliebe [a love of order], but the presence of these local
officials soon became intrusive and intimidating. One would
routinely glance to left and right before making any remarks
that might be interpreted as critical of the regime, especially
in public places, a habit that was commonly known as the
'German glance'.

Promotion to block warden gave these individuals power
over their neighbours and many evidently took pleasure in
exercising that authority. In the province of Hesse-Nessau
alone there were 33,165 official informers on the party
payroll (see: Thomas Berger, *Lebenssituationen unter der
Herrschaft des Nationalsozialismus*).

The German writer Bernt Engelmann cites an example of
how the regime encouraged its citizens to become complicit
in its crimes. An acquaintance identified only by his first
name, Kulle, told the writer of the time his father felt he had

By 1938, the victimization of Jewish communities and the destruction of their businesses was so commonplace that many German citizens did not find it remarkable.

no option but to inform on a complete stranger to save himself from coming under suspicion. It was the summer of 1935, and Kulle's family were staying at a hotel where the father fell into conversation with another guest, a painter by profession. The two men enjoyed 'very interesting discussions' during their stay, at the end of which the other man left Herr Kulle a newspaper he had been reading. It was an anti-Nazi newspaper that had been published in Paris and Herr Kulle feared that a pro-Nazi couple had seen him looking at it. He had no doubt that they would report him at the earliest opportunity, judging from the enthusiastic 'Heil Hitler!' with which they had greeted him each morning. So he hastily crumpled it up and affected outrage at having been duped into reading it. His quick thinking probably saved him as his fellow guest was an *Untersturmfuhrer* in the SS, who immediately reported the incident to the Gestapo. The painter was arrested.

Kulle never learned what became of him, but he believed that it was only by denouncing a stranger that his father had averted suspicion from himself and saved his job and perhaps also his life.

Moral Self-Mutilation

The Nazis did not outlaw free speech overnight. Censorship came surreptitiously at first. Foreign newspapers became harder to come by. Those who trusted *The Times* to give them an unbiased account of international events, for example, found themselves making an increased effort to be first at the kiosk when the morning editions were delivered. Within a short time, news from abroad became as rare as real coffee, and there was also a risk of arrest for anyone found listening to foreign broadcasts.

The official reason for this regulation was typical of Nazi double-think. They called it *moralische Selbstverstümmelung* [moral self-mutilation], meaning the deliberate lowering of one's morale by listening to enemy propaganda. But those who desired the facts thought it worth the risk of five years' imprisonment and listened with their ear to the speaker. Even that was perilous as children were known to tell their parents that a friend had remarked that his or her mother or father listened to the radio the same way. It took only a care-less remark like that within earshot of a zealous party member and offenders could find themselves invited to explain their actions at Gestapo headquarters.

Under such circumstances, rumour and hearsay became

the main source of news. There were ludicrous tales to tease the gullible, specifically that some of the Nazi leaders were Jews (Goebbels, Rosenberg and Ley being frequently mentioned in this regard) and more sinister stories concerning what awaited those who were arrested under the so-called 'Night and Fog' decree in the newly built concentration camp at Dachau on the outskirts of Munich.

It was only when ordinary Germans were personally confronted with the consequences of the regime's decrees and directives that they understood the human cost of living in a dictatorship.

For Christabel Bielenberg this occurred the night one of her children was struck with a serious fever. Her Jewish doctor was summoned and spent all night tending the boy, which was unusual as he had previously been very busy. But she had noticed that it had become easier to make an appointment or request a house call in recent months. As the doctor was leaving that morning he asked if Frau Bielenberg wished him to continue to look after the child and when she asked why he would say such a thing, he told her that he had been ordered to close his practice and that he had received threatening letters warning him not to treat Aryan children. Instead, she was advised not to use the telephone but to come to the clinic or his apartment in person when she needed to make an appointment. The next time she did so she discovered that he had departed for Holland with no prospect of employment and that he had left all his belongings behind.

Two years later she heard from his housekeeper that he had died suddenly. Some said it was suicide, but Christabel suspected otherwise.

Her husband Peter had his suspicions confirmed regarding

the regime when he was asked to defend a Social Democrat accused of distributing illegal leaflets. No sooner had Peter offered a spirited defence that resulted in the acquittal of his client than the man was arrested under the pretext euphemistically termed 'protective custody' and bundled into an unmarked van that drove off at speed. Fruitless efforts to discover the man's whereabouts at police headquarters and the disinterested shrugs that met all his enquiries finally convinced the young lawyer that eight years of legal training had been in vain. Peter's father had worked all his life in order to be able to hand a flourishing legal practice over to his son and now it was to be abandoned. But even more disheartening was the realization that he had been defeated by a government which openly flouted the law and was in flagrant violation of basic human rights.

'Efficient intimidation can only be achieved either by capital punishment or by measures by which the relatives of the criminal and the population do not know his fate.'
(General Keitel's defence of the 'Night and Fog' decree at Nuremberg, 1946)

Sign of the Times

'No class or group or party in Germany could escape its share of responsibility for the abandonment of the democratic Republic and the advent of Adolf Hitler. The cardinal error of the Germans who opposed Nazism was their failure to unite against it.'
(William L. Shirer, *The Rise and Fall of the Thrid Reich: A History of Nazi Germany*)

If any of Germany's foreign 'friends', as they liked to style themselves – those who openly admired Hitler and defended Germany's right to rearm in defiance of the Versailles Treaty – chose to show their support by visiting the country in the years after Hitler became chancellor, they would have seen unmistakable signs that the Greater Reich was a totalitarian state.

Public parks, facilities and cafés bore signs prohibiting Jews, while other notices forbade women from smoking in public (SA men were known to snatch cigarettes from the mouths of any women caught smoking, stub them out and reprimand them for insulting the Führer, who did not approve of the habit).

Every opportunity was seized upon to demonstrate one's National Socialist zeal and allegiance to the party by imposing rules and regulations. Hotels and apartment blocks displayed notices informing residents that it was their duty to display the Nazi flag on the Führer's birthday. Many shops, restaurants and cafés put up prominent warnings to customers that the required greeting was 'Heil Hitler!' Anything other than total compliance would be interpreted as disloyalty.

The infamous Nuremberg Laws of 1935 – which deprived Jews of their citizenship, prohibited them from marrying or having a sexual relationship with gentiles and excluded them from working in the civil service and other professions – was justified by the need to 'clarify' their status in German society. A Jew was deemed to be anyone who had three or more Jewish grandparents, regardless of whether they were religiously observant or had intermarried. The measures that Hitler described as 'a definitive legal adjustment' were accepted with relief by some Jews, who hoped they might allow them to remain in Germany, albeit as second-class citizens, and that they might finally put an end to the anti-Semitic attacks, arrests and boycotts of Jewish businesses.

Night of Broken Glass

For those politicians who had hoped the 'excesses' of the regime might be reined in once they had taken their seats in the Reichstag, there was a rude awakening on the morning of 10 November 1938. The previous night, which came to be known as *Kristallnacht*, or the 'Night of Broken Glass', saw Nazi hooligans smashing shops and business premises belonging to Jews and burning synagogues in towns and cities throughout Germany, Austria and the Sudetenland. These supposedly 'spontaneous' acts of vandalism were said to be in retaliation for the assassination of a German embassy official in Paris, but they had in fact been instigated by Goebbels and orchestrated by Reinhard Heydrich, assistant to SS Reichsführer Himmler.

Some lowered their eyes and hurried past the boarded-up windows. A few expressed their disgust under their breath and hoped they wouldn't be overheard. It was a shame on the German nation and the work of the rabble. What must other nations be thinking of the Germans now? Some noted the destruction with smug satisfaction and thought that it was about time these Jews were shown that they weren't welcome. Whatever their views, from that moment on it was impossible for the citizens of Germany to deny the criminal nature of the regime. Those who naively hoped that such shameful acts might awaken those with a conscience and encourage them to take action were cruelly disappointed.

The dictatorship had a stranglehold on free speech, which was enforced by terror and intimidation. There was nothing one could do to voice disapproval.

Berlin housewife Emmi Bonhoefer was contemptuous of those who denied all knowledge of the dictatorship's persecution of the Jews and other minorities:

'Of course in '38 when the synagogues were burning everybody knew what was going on. I remember my brother-in-law told me that he went to his office by train the morning after Kristallnacht and between the stations of Zarienplatz and zoological gardens there was a Jewish synagogue on fire and he murmured, "That's a shame on our culture." Right away a gentleman sitting opposite him turned his lapel and showed his party badge and produced his papers showing he was Gestapo. My brother-in-law had to show his papers and give his address and was ordered to come to the party office next morning at 9 o'clock. He was questioned and had to explain what he had meant by that remark. He tried to talk himself out of it but his punishment was that he had to arrange and distribute the ration cards for the area at the beginning of every month. And he did this for seven years until the end of the war. The family had to arrange the cards for each category of the population, workers, children etc. but he was not permitted to have a helper. He had to go alone. That was how they broke the back of the people.'

Not everyone turned a blind eye, or lowered their gaze and acted as if nothing untoward had occurred. Johann Stab was a police officer on duty in the town of Kleinheubach on 9 November 1938, and while it is not clear from his report that

SA thugs were a familiar presence on German streets. Their actions often directly contravened German law, until the laws were changed and mob rule was legitimized.

he acted to protect the Jewish residents out of compassion, or simply to maintain law and order, it is notable that he did not allow the SA 'thugs' as he called them to intimidate him or interfere with the carrying out of his duty. When he reported the disturbances to his superior officer in nearby Miltenberg, he was told that it was not something he need concern himself with and that everything was under control. However, Stab was dissatisfied with this assurance and went to investigate.

In the main square he found that a small group of brown shirts had forced their way into the home of a Jewish resident and had begun to vandalize the property. He managed to persuade them to leave by informing them that the house had been sold to an Aryan buyer and that they were now damaging property it was his duty to protect. He was told that the group had broken into other Jewish homes and businesses and thrown furniture, possessions and goods into the street. But he was then ordered not to make arrests or to interfere. Where the order had originated he had no idea, but his superior officer was adamant that the acts of destruction had been officially sanctioned and were not to be questioned.

Later that same evening, he received further orders to take all Jewish residents into 'protective custody', but before doing so Stab locked all the damaged properties and posted an SA man outside each one to prevent further damage or looting. He then found himself arguing against the forced detainment of the female owner of a local shoe shop who was ill and confined to bed. The SA insisted that she be dragged out of her sick bed and taken to prison, but Stab was adamant that if she was to be moved at all it would be to a hospital. After much argument he managed to persuade two of them to accompany him to the woman's home where they found her clearly unwell and visibly terrified. She was 'a truly pitiful sight', sufficiently sick to convince the SA to leave her be, for the time being.

Professor Tubach, a former member of the Hitler Youth who came to despise the Nazis and after the war co-authored *An Uncommon Friendship* with a Holocaust survivor, interviewed a woman who had witnessed the aftermath of *Kristallnacht* from the safety of her classroom. She recalled that her teacher had interrupted his class to take the pupils outside to see a burning synagogue ringed with SA thugs who prevented the fire brigade from intervening. No comment was made during or after the unscheduled outing, which can be interpreted as either shameful indifference or a general feeling that the Jews had finally got what they deserved.

Jews were not the only victims of the boycott and the repercussions of *Kristallnacht*. Their Aryan employees lost their livelihoods and the older workers frequently had to take menial, low-paying jobs that crushed their self-esteem. The fact that they had worked for a Jewish business could count against them, and if they also had affiliations with opposition parties, the authorities could see to it that they were dismissed from their new post. In such cases the only option was to find *Schwarzarbeit* [illicit unregistered employment].

Political opponents, those who had been members of the banned opposition parties, were also marginalized by the Nazis. Hans-Bernhard Schunemann had been a member of the Hitler Youth, but his father had refused to join the party. Consequently, Herr Schunemann found himself demoted to technical director of his own printing firm and a Nazi was put in charge to ensure that the presses were not used to print anything that could be construed as being critical of the regime.

Goebbels' Snout

Radio, or wireless as it was called then, was a luxury until the regime introduced the state-subsidized *Volksempfänger* [people's receiver] to ensure that everyone heard the official party broadcasts. This ensured that '80 million people were deprived of independent thought,' according to armaments minister Albert Speer.

The first two-band sets sold for about half the price of

their competitors but could receive signals only from local and regional stations, ensuring that listeners could not tune in to broadcasts from overseas. The cheapest model sold for just 35 Reich marks and was popularly referred to as 'Goebbels' snout'. By 1939, it was estimated that 70 per cent of German homes possessed a radio.

The state broadcaster RBC offered a limited programme of propaganda talks interspersed with *völkische* folk music and selective classical pieces (no jazz or Jewish composers), which it was difficult to avoid as the new wireless was a fixture in many workplaces and public bars and cafés.

Both radio and newsprint journalists were vetted and their work had to be submitted to the state-controlled press agency, the DNB, for approval before publication. Criticism of the regime was forbidden as Hitler made clear in a speech to journalists on 10 November 1938:

'What is necessary is that the press blindly follow the basic principle: the leadership is always right!'

As minister for propaganda and enlightenment, Goebbels demanded tight editorial control of all publications. These included 3,600 newspapers and several hundred magazines. His memo to editors dated 22 October 1936 was typical of the thinly veiled threats he issued on an almost weekly basis:

'It turns out time and again that news and background stories still appear in the German press, which drip with an almost suicidal objectivity and which are simply irrespon-sible. What is not desired is newspapers edited in the old Liberalistic spirit. What is desired is that newspapers be brought in line with the basic tenets of building the

National Socialist state.'

The cinema, which had only recently found its voice after the conversion from silent to sound, was also harnessed by the regime for propaganda purposes, most effectively in Veit Harlan's inflammatory anti-Semitic melodrama *Jud Süss* (1940) and in Leni Riefenstahl's two technically impressive documentaries *Triumph of the Will* (1935) and *Olympia* (1936). The former documented the quasi-religious ritual of the annual Nuremberg Party Rally, while the latter portrayed Aryan athletic heroes as if they were gods of antiquity. However, Goebbels was shrewd enough to realize that the audience would not stand for too much proselytizing and so sweetened his message by commissioning frothy romantic comedies and melodramas that sentimentalized the self-sacrificing mother and idealized the German *heimat* [loosely, the homeland]. But outside in the real world the picture was far less pleasant.

Chapter Five
The Storm Breaks

The Onset of War

For the ordinary German, the Second World War did not begin with the hellish screaming of Stuka dive bombers and ground-shaking explosions, as it did for the civilians of Warsaw and Krakow. There were no air-raid drills or black-outs as there were in Britain, or panic buying of essential foodstuffs and petrol as there was in France, Belgium and the Netherlands. Instead, the first sign that Germany was now engaged in an international conflict came with the severing of all communication with the outside world. From the after-noon of 1 September 1939, no phone calls could be made outside of the Reich. Operators were instructed to inform callers that they were unable to connect them, but that normal service would be resumed as soon as possible.

The wireless was now people's primary source of informa-tion and all broadcasts had to be approved by Goebbels' Ministry of Propaganda and Public Enlightenment. Consequently, the tone of the first news announcements on the eve of war was one of resignation and resolve. It was 'regrettable' that events had come to this, but the leadership

had a 'clear conscience'. The German people had a right to
Lebensraum [living space]:

> **'We have done all that any country could do to
> establish peace.'**

Few who listened to the news on that mild autumn evening
would have questioned that right. For more than a year the
population of Germany and its Axis allies had been conditioned to believe that they were the victims of the vindictive
Allied powers who had imposed punitive reparations after
Germany's defeat in the First World War and who had occupied territory that the Führer had declared to be sacred soil.
The invasion of Poland was not an act of aggression, they
were told, but merely Germany exercising its authority to
'liberate' German nationals from the occupied territories and
to cleanse Europe of 'inferior races' so that Eastern Europe
could be Aryanized.

When war was declared, one of the first adjustments
everyone had to get used to was the blackout. Ordinary
blinds were insufficient, as the population was reminded in
no uncertain terms by the officious block wardens and the
police, who served a penalty notice on anyone allowing even
a chink of light to escape.

The sombre mood across the country was in stark
contrast to the drum-beating patriotism that had greeted
the declaration of war in 1918. There was also much
grumbling and discontentment, particularly in the rural
communities, which would see many older men from
peasant families – some over 40 – being drafted while a
sizeable number of young men were given exemption from

Ethnic Germans living in territories ceded under the terms of the Versailles Treaty were particularly loyal to the Führer and attracted to his policy of racial cleansing. Here Hitler is seen returning the Nazi salute to the thousands of citizens in the former free city of Danzig who turned out to welcome him.

military service on the grounds that they were in valued professions. These exceptions created a 'pervasive mood of poisonous resentment' among the population according to one official report.

But if German civilians imagined that the war would be confined to the battlefields and that early victories in Poland, France, Belgium and the Netherlands would bring peace and prosperity on the home front, they were soon disillusioned. Rationing and shortages were just two of the many inconveniences imposed on the German hausfrau in the early months of the war.

They quickly learned that the only way to acquire certain foodstuffs was either to start early and scour the market stalls for fresh produce or to ingratiate themselves with the local shopkeepers and farmers and to set aside any qualms they might have about putting the welfare of their own family before the community as the propaganda posters urged them to do. '*Gemeinnutz geht vor Eigennutz*' [community welfare before self-interest] was the slogan that reminded them of their civic duty as they joined the queue for items for which they had no immediate use, but that they thought might be necessary in the future.

Rationing was a hardship one got used to, but it was exacerbated by the fact that rations were reduced as time and the war wore on. Even the most house-proud suburban hausfrau considered erecting an inconspicuous henhouse or chicken coup in her backyard in the hope of replacing powdered egg with the real thing. And if the birds weren't productive, at least they would make a decent dinner.

In the spring of 1940, when Germans were supposedly basking in the glow of a succession of swift victories and Hitler was reported to be sightseeing in Paris, German mothers were praying that the rumours of a peace treaty with Britain was imminent so that their menfolk could come home. If asked, they would say they still believed in ultimate victory, but in the meantime they would put their faith in the black market and make do with *Sparrezepte* [economy recipes] and *Suppengrun*, a clump of vegetable stalks tied together with string that was said to make nourishing vegetable soup.

Food rationing was adequate at first but then the grocers and butchers found ways to profit by it without arousing suspicion. The easiest way was for them to tamper with the scales so that they could measure out a few grams less than the allowance. By the close of business each day the shop owner or sales assistant would have enough left over to sell or trade on the black market. Another trick they perfected was throwing the produce onto the scale and lifting it off before it could settle and register the weight. No one dared to complain for fear of being told to take their custom elsewhere.

'Guns, not butter'

The first flush of nationalist fever that had attended Hitler's succession to the chancellorship and the series of bloodless coups that saw occupied territory absorbed into the Reich faded after food shortages and the scarcity of essential materials began to hit home. The Nazis' 'guns, not butter' policy (announced by Goering in a speech he made in 1934) resulted in rationing in all but name, while the textile shortage created by the restriction on British imports in 1938 forced many Germans to face the fact that allegiance to the regime came at the cost of many basic items they had taken for granted.

Ladies were denied the luxury of imported French perfume and fashions (although the wives of Nazi officials ordered them regardless) and men found that even tailored suits were inferior to those cut from bolts of English cloth. Whereas once they could have expected a well-made suit to last for years, the German equivalent lasted barely a season, giving rise to the saying that 'German Forest' brand suits swelled in the spring and changed colour in the autumn.

Rationing was officially introduced on 28 August 1939 and limited the amount of basic foodstuffs, such as bread, flour, meat, cheese, sugar and jam, as well as shoes, soap, leather goods and coal. Even tea and coffee were soon in short supply and almost every essential item had risen in price by the end of that year.

By the winter of 1940 many German civilians were relying on handouts from the *Volkswohlfahrt* [people's welfare], the state-sponsored organization that had been founded to dispense charity to the destitute. Its Christmas package for that year contained what were already regarded as rare treats – a quarter-pound of cocoa, a kilo of lard and a handful of sweets. Some of the younger children had never seen or tasted chocolate.

By the time the Wehrmacht had suffered its first serious defeat at Stalingrad in February 1943, Germans were reduced to swapping clothing coupons for food stamps and drinking ersatz coffee – a vile watery solution made from roasted barley that reminded them of the sacrifices they were making for waging Hitler's war.

Tobacco, too, was obtainable only with special smokers' cards marked M for men and W for women, with the latter entitled to half the men's allocation. Hitler's disapproval of women smokers had apparently been circumvented on the grounds that many were now working in the armaments factories and other branches of the armed forces in a clerical capacity and needed a boost that only nicotine could offer them.

Shortages, longer working hours and drives for more productivity were largely tolerated while the German armed forces were advancing across Western Europe, the Balkans, North Africa and Russia. Imminent victory then seemed assured, but from the winter of 1942 the mood at home became considerably less optimistic. Hope of a swift victory evaporated after the shocking defeat of Rommel's

Afrika Korps at the second battle of El Alamein in November 1942. Soon after, German civilians were informed of the fate facing the once invincible Wehrmacht on the Eastern Front and asked to make further sacrifices to provide winter clothing for the Sixth Army that was besieged at Stalingrad.

News of their ignominious surrender in February 1943 was all the more demoralizing because it had followed assurances from the Ministry of Propaganda that the Soviet forces had been on the verge of collapse. But although these reversals had a significant impact on morale, it was the intensity of the Allied bombing raids on German cities that brought the gravity of the situation home to the civilian population. Each month brought more bad news that even Goebbels was hard pressed to deny, or to present as a strategic withdrawal. When news of the loss of more than 40 U-boats in May of 1943 forced Admiral Dönitz to withdraw his 'wolfpacks' from the Battle of the Atlantic, every German knew it meant that the Allied convoys would be largely unmolested from now on while their own supply ships would be at the mercy of Allied warships and fighters.

By war's end, many adults were reduced to eating horsemeat, if they were lucky enough to find it, but even starvation and the threat of being besieged on all sides failed to shake some diehard Nazis. The mood inside Hitler's Germany was grim but determined. It was summed up by a slogan that was being scrawled on the walls of bombed-out buildings throughout the country:

'Enjoy the war. Peace will be hell.'

The Darkening Storm

The mood had darkened considerably with the first Allied air raids on major German cities in the summer of 1941, and it deteriorated from then on. US correspondent William L. Shirer noted the reaction of Berliners to the first raid on the capital on August 26:

'The Berliners are stunned. They did not think it could ever happen. When this war began, Goering assured them it couldn't ... They believed him. Their disillusionment today therefore is all the greater. You have to see their faces to measure it.'

But while the British were said to have pulled together and put on a brave face during the Blitz, the Germans were prone to schadenfreude, with the citizens of Hamburg and the Rhineland taking a small amount of satisfaction from the fact that it was now the turn of the arrogant Berliners to cower in their shelters under the impact of British bombs.

As time went on, however, the raids had less impact and became almost routine, to be endured like a severe winter storm. The population as a whole steeled themselves to survive at all costs and became less inquisitive about their neighbours' politics and party loyalties and more concerned about seeing it through together.

In this stifling atmosphere of suspicion and scepticism, crime flourished, despite the omniscient presence of the secret police. In the blackout, cases of rape and murder rose alarmingly, giving lie to the belief that crime would fall under a totalitarian regime. Rationing gave rise to a thriving black market in forged coupons, the theft of rationed provisions from government warehouses and general racketeering. Drug dealers, draft dodgers and other opportunists on the fringes of the criminal underworld were forced deeper underground to take advantage of a phantom economy born of austerity. This invisible population was enlarged by between 5,000 and 7,000 Jews, who were in hiding from the authorities (commonly known as 'submarines'). One such individual was Cioma Schönhaus.

The Forger

In June 1942, 20-year-old Berliner Cioma Schönhaus escaped deportation to a concentration camp because he was more valuable to the Reich as a skilled worker in one of their munitions factories. His parents and family were sent to their deaths at Majdanek extermination camp near Lublin, and Cioma was left to fend for himself. A German acquaintance had told the boy, 'It is irresponsible to pull away from the evacuation. All Jews must suffer together. All must go together. One has to obey and do what the authorities request.' Cioma's reply was, 'They can kiss my ass. I won't let myself get caught. I want to be free.'

Remarkably, in the very centre of Hitler's web, he chanced upon Germans who were willing to risk their lives to help an 'enemy of the state'. The factory foreman told him how to sabotage the machine-gun barrels that he was filing and a former government minister offered to supply him with false identity papers when it became necessary for him to disappear into the underground community of escaped Jews and other 'undesirables' living in the sewers and deserted buildings of the capital.

There Cioma survived working as a document forger, using the skills he had learned at art school to alter identity cards and passbooks for fellow 'submarines'. He also created multiple identities for himself so that he could live in a number of apartments unmolested by the Gestapo and occasionally eat in expensive restaurants that were off-limits to Jews. These included the Kaiserhof, a favourite restaurant of Hitler, Himmler and Goebbels. So he was frequently in the midst of Nazi officials – indeed, where better to hide than among the very people looking for him? He admits it gave him an adrenaline rush to defy his tormentors in this way and it became addictive.

Though obliged to wear the Yellow Star on his coat to identify himself as a Jew, he simply adapted it so that he could snap it off when entering a prohibited area and stick it back on when the police were conducting an inspection.

The ever-present threat of discovery was alleviated by his mordant humour as well as by a certain frisson he felt from playing cat and mouse with the Gestapo. After the Gestapo sealed the rooms of members of his family who had been transported to the gas chambers, Cioma prised them open, took whatever valuables he could find to sell on the black market and sealed them back up.

He also kept up his spirits by holding imaginary conversations with his dead father, who told him:

'In spite of the goods trains you must say "yes" to life. As our representative you have a duty to experience all the pleasures we were denied.'

He was aided in his efforts by Protestant members of the

Confessing Church, a resistance group who believed that it was their Christian duty to help Jews evade Nazi persecution. They would turn their identity papers over to Cioma, who would copy them for other 'illegals', then they'd claim they had lost them. They did so knowing the risk they were taking. Some were arrested and executed.

But the hardest part was simply finding a place to live. Putting on a brave front, he marched into a government office and asked for a list of landlords after claiming that he had been forced to surrender his own apartment to a relative who had been bombed out of his home in another city.

He slept at each address in turn, arriving in the evening when it was too late to register with the police and leaving first thing in the morning after claiming that he had just received his army call-up papers.

It was only when the former government minister Herr Kaufmann offered to supply him with false identity papers that Cioma decided his incredible run of luck might have been about to run out. On 6 September 1943, he packed a rucksack and pedalled across Berlin on his bike on the long ride towards the Swiss border, a copy of a book by Dr Goebbels in his rucksack in case he was stopped and questioned. A forged service record enabled him to stay in hotels and eat in cafés without attracting the attention of the authorities. He attributed his incredible good fortune to the fact that he remained unsentimental:

> *'When you are sad, it is like having a stone around your neck and you can no longer take action. You are lost.'*

Danger and Despair

But by the spring of 1944 the average German was beginning to despair of being alive to see the end of the war. Whether it would be victory or surrender, many had ceased to care. They desired only for it to end so that they could resume their lives without the constant threat of bombardment. It wasn't only the night-time air raids that disrupted the daily routine. Every journey was fraught with danger, especially after D-Day, when the Luftwaffe were effectively grounded and the Allies were free to strafe civilian and military transport all across Germany. Some Allied pilots had become proficient at puncturing engines to immobilize locomotives, blocking the line and thus preventing other trains from getting through.

But although the structural damage to the intended targets was often minimal, the impact on German morale was considerable. Goering had boasted that no Allied bombs would fall on Berlin while his invincible Luftwaffe ruled the skies and when he was proven wrong, it gave the population cause to question what other lies they were being told.

Night after night, the Allies pounded munitions factories and aircraft engine works, and the next morning the official German broadcasts would claim that another school or hospital had been hit by the Allied 'air pirates'. But while the besieged Brits were free to turn off Lord Haw-Haw's German propaganda broadcasts, German civilians were required to tune in to folksy fireside sermons by Dr Hans Fritzsche, who urged parents to buy their children Christmas presents handmade from leather coats rather than toys, to support the fighting men on the Eastern Front. Few were persuaded – especially when faced with pleading children who didn't care a fig for patriotism.

As late as spring 1944, the German press continued to proclaim victory in two-inch-high headlines. When they finally acknowledged that their troops were making steady progress on the Eastern Front despite difficult circumstances, only the most staunch believer in the invincibility of the master race could fail to interpret it as an admission that the Russian campaign was not proceeding according to plan.

Soon every retreat became a strategic withdrawal. But the true picture of what was occurring inside Germany was to be found in the inside pages of the *Völkischer Beobachter* and its regional rivals. The implacable discipline that held Germany together under the supreme will of the Führer was beginning to crack. The unpalatable facts were to be read in the reports of the latest 'criminal' to be found guilty and summarily executed after a phoney trial for undermining the morale of the people. Invariably their 'crime' was inconsequential – the minor theft of provisions or a violation of a blackout regulation.

The message was clear: disloyalty was punishable by death.

The very thought of defeat was treasonable. And yet an increasing number of sons, brothers and fathers were coming home on leave to tell their families what they had witnessed in the east. Care-worn and weary, more than one had warned that the Russians would not be merciful after what their people had suffered under the advancing German army.

Wartime Love

While German film-makers depicted an impossibly idyllic life on the home front, not all of the country's young women

A still from *Wunschkonzert*, a hugely popular propaganda film from 1940, in which two Luftwaffe pilots fall in love with the same girl. The theme was a staple of American war films of the period and was reworked some 60 years later for the Jerry Bruckheimer blockbuster *Pearl Harbor* (2001).

suffered separation as graciously as the heroines of two of the most popular pictures of the period, *Wunschkonzert* (1940) and *Die Grosse Liebe* (1942), both of which dealt with lovers separated by the war. The constant threat of Allied bombing, the absence of their husband or lovers and the dreariness of wartime rationing and restrictions led many German women to seek the company of other men.

In the rural districts where foreign prisoners were billeted on farms, the fresh-faced symbol of Aryan motherhood often cast aside her reservations and political ideals when a suitable male companion was available, regardless of his ethnic origins. Even the threat of imprisonment was not sufficient to deter them, with the consequence that the illegitimacy rate increased five-fold in the last year of the war to 20 per cent of all registered births.

The German mother's hardship was exacerbated by the worry of having to provide for her children when there was little food to be had. But it was preferable to being separated from both her man and her child, as many were in the last two years of the war, when 1.7 million children aged between 6 and 14 were evacuated from German towns and cities under threat of Allied air attack. A further half a million children were evacuated with their mothers.

The fortunate ones found refuge with relatives, but the majority were billeted with strangers in rural areas, who resented the intruders and begrudged them anything more than the bare necessities. The city mothers tended to be seen as lazy and self-centred because many were unwilling to work as they had to care for their children, or they worked only the bare minimum for the same reason.

Berlin mother Christabel Bielenberg was acutely aware of how fortunate she was to have been offered accommodation away from the constant threat of air raids, but she was nevertheless weary of living in spare bedrooms, scrounging for food and apologizing for her children, who would misbehave from sheer boredom or because they missed their father and the familiar surroundings of home.

Some children were surprisingly resilient and resourceful, playing war games among the rubble or assuming responsibility for cheering up their mothers. One little girl knowingly exploited her starved appearance to forage for food from sympathetic farmers' wives, while a young boy found a talent for doing deals on the black market to supplement his mother's meagre income. But the majority were distressed by being separated from their parents and some were deliberately ill-treated or neglected by their reluctant hosts.

Fathers too were forcibly separated from their wives and children by the war, whether they were serving in the armed forces or working for the state in some other capacity. Some who didn't qualify for leave or who were unable to obtain it, suffered as much as their partners. First Lieutenant Werner L. from Krefeld wrote to his two-year-old daughter:

'You and your mother are going through the wonderful early stages of childhood and motherhood without me. I am still among soldiers, as I was two years ago when we knew you were on the way.'

Wunschkonzerts, the weekly forces' request programmes broadcast on the radio every Sunday night, offered the illusion of togetherness as soldiers' letters to loved ones back home were read out. These were interspersed with popular songs that they or their sweethearts and family had requested, but they were no substitute for a personal letter that could be read over and over again.

Letters Home

'As much normality as possible, as much war as necessary.'

(Nazi slogan)

During the course of the Second World War, 18 million German men left home to serve in the armed forces. For the majority of two-parent families this meant that the children were left in the care of their mother, or a female relative, friend or neighbour if the mother was unwilling or unable to give up her job. It is debatable whether this enforced separation from their husbands and partners made many of those women more independent and self-reliant. But a large proportion of the 30 million-plus letters written to and from the Home Front between 1939 and 1945 reveal that privation, suffering and the absence of a partner attested to the durability of the traditional family unit, even under such extreme conditions. And this despite the fact that 11 million German soldiers were detained in Russian POW camps for many years after the war ended. For some this extended into the mid-1950s.

The letters unearthed in the archives of the German postal service by researchers and historians are, on the whole, surprisingly lacking in sentiment and instead focus on practical advice given by husbands to their wives, encouraging them to bear up and be patient until they can be reunited. They urge their children not to neglect their school work, to help their mothers and to keep their spirits up.

The need to write and unburden oneself of pent-up feelings would not be stemmed, even when communications were severely disrupted or there was little chance of the letter being delivered. At such times many women confided their hopes and fears in the pages of their diaries. Beate K., a 23-year-old wife and mother from Königsberg, conveyed the strain of bringing up a child alone:

With millions of German men drafted into the armed forces for the duration of the war, children were left in the care of their mother or a female relative, friend or neighbour.

'It would be so lovely if only your father were here ...
Sometimes it is horribly difficult to keep going.'

Few servicemen expressed any opinions regarding the regime or the outcome of the war as every soldier was aware of the rigid censorship imposed on correspondence from the front. It was common practice for soldiers' letters to be tested for invisible ink and any form of code (even the innocuous codes used by lovers) was forbidden. The Nazi leadership was so fearful that captured German soldiers might be susceptible to Soviet propaganda that the Reich security office confiscated 20,000 letters written by German POWs, which remained undelivered at the end of the war.

Chapter Six
Witnesses

An Unconventional Family

Eycke Strickland was born in Kassel in the heart of Germany nine months after Hitler was appointed chancellor. Her 'unconventional' parents, Auguste and Karl Laabs, were pacifists on principle – her father having served in Flanders during the First World War, where he saw his older brother killed before his eyes, and Eycke's maternal grandfather having fallen on the battlefield despite his wife's fervent prayers for his safe return.

Both parents grew up to be self-reliant and somewhat suspicious of extreme nationalism. They had met through a German Youth movement called the *Wandervogel*, which instilled a love of nature in its rather idealistic members and espoused egalitarian values that Auguste and Karl in turn imparted to their children.

Karl was barred from completing his doctorate in economics and social sciences after writing a critical anti-Nazi slogan on the blackboard of a lecture hall on the day Hitler acceded to the chancellorship, and he took a job as an architect. The family settled in Wilhelmshausen, a small village north of Kassel, where Karl designed affordable houses for workers who would otherwise have been forced to live in crowded tenements.

By August 1939, on the eve of war, Eycke, her two brothers and younger sister were uprooted and moved to Vaake, another small village in Hesse, where their parents thought the family would be safer. Immediately they began preparing their small garden to grow their own food but before the planting could begin Karl was drafted to do civilian duty building airfield installations for the Luftwaffe far from home. Shortly afterwards, Auguste left the children in the care of a maid while she appeared in court to defend herself on a charge of insulting a member of the party while protesting on her husband's behalf.

But it was only the beginning of their troubles. In July 1940 Eycke's younger sister, Ute, developed pleurisy and was admitted to a children's hospital where she was treated successfully. But when the day came for her to return home, all of the children, including the contagious patients, were rushed into a bomb shelter during an air raid and Ute was infected with diphtheria and died shortly afterwards. Her parents went into mourning; her mother wore a black dress every day for a year and her father a black armband. It wasn't long before Eycke noticed that there were more women dressed in black and men wearing black armbands in the village.

However, it was not until 1941 that 7-year-old Eycke learned that 30 January had significance for someone other than her father, who celebrated his birthday on that day.

Her teacher explained that it was a national holiday because on that day eight years earlier the Führer had been appointed chancellor. At assembly that morning the hall was decorated with red and white flags and the children were told that the symbol in the centre was called a swastika. After listening to a speech extolling the virtues of National Socialism and their own privileged part as citizens of the new Germany, the class was told that they were expected to learn the words of 'Deutschland über Alles' so that they could sing it at the next assembly. Their indoctrination had begun. And yet there was something inside Eycke that prevented her from giving the Hitler salute whenever the *Bonzen* [petty bureaucrats] of the village appeared.

But Eycke's story only truly began in March 1942 when the family moved to Poland to be with their father, who was employed as the county architect in Krenau, a few miles west of a town that was to become synonymous with the Holocaust – Auschwitz.

It was in Krenau that Karl met Mordecai Hartmann, a young Jewish man who worked as a stoker in his office building and who introduced the 'unconventional' German to his family. From them, Eycke's father learned of the fate that awaited the Jews of Poland and in befriending them he resolved that he must do all he could to save as many as possible, whatever the risk to himself and his family.

For Eycke and her siblings, the 7-acre farm with its barns and outbuildings seemed like a children's paradise. They were free to play and explore, and treated the livestock as if it were their private zoo. It was only when their father erected a new fence to keep their feathered friends in and the 'troublemakers' out that Eycke wondered if it might not be the home she had always dreamed of.

No mention had been made of the previous owners, but when the duck pond was drained it threw up a short-wave radio that they must have been in a hurry to hide. Auguste ordered Mordecai to bury it and swore him to secrecy. Some time after that another incident aroused Eycke's curiosity. While out riding in an open buggy with her father she was approached by a well-dressed man who exchanged greetings with her father and then offered him a handmade Kathe Kruse doll for his daughter. The doll was much valued by collectors and would have been a rare gift for a child, but to Eycke's astonishment her father rejected it curtly saying, 'You know I cannot accept your gift. Goodbye, Herr Goldmann.' From the look on his face, Herr Goldmann was as shocked as she had been. Her father was not the kind to deny his daughter a gift from a well-meaning acquaintance and when Eycke asked him why he hadn't allowed her to accept it, he told her only, 'Eyes are watching, ears are listening', and motioned towards the driver of their buggy. The following Christmas Eycke saw her younger sister cradling it and learned that her mother had found it one day sitting abandoned on the gate post. Herr Goldmann had found a solution that did not bring suspicion on the family.

It was only much later, after the war, that her father felt he was able to tell Eycke why he had had to be careful not to be seen accepting gifts from a Jewish friend. As *Kreisbaurat* [county architect] he was responsible for issuing work permits that guaranteed food, pay and safe passage for labourers employed on municipal projects. At great risk to himself he had given priority to Jews, who were in constant threat of being transported to forced labour or extermination camps. On several occasions, dozens of the men and women on her father's list had been rounded up for transportation after a Jewish policeman had crossed their names off the list and substituted others who had presumably bribed him in an effort to save themselves. When Karl learned of it, he stormed off to the assembly area with his list and demanded that his workers be released immediately. Through bluff and bluster he managed to persuade a Gestapo official that he couldn't complete the projects without his workers and they were released.

Interview with Eycke Strickland

Eycke graciously agreed to be interviewed for this book. She asked that her answers be preceded by this comment:

'Since I am not qualified to speak for the German people, I shall limit most of my answers to what I saw and heard as a child.'

What did your parents tell you about life in Germany prior to Hitler?

Only that the years after the First World War were especially hard for my mother's family after her father was killed at the first Battle of Langemarck in Belgium. Chaos, starvation, inflation, civil unrest, lawlessness and a deep resentment on account of the Versailles Treaty reigned, as one after another the Weimar Republic governments failed to solve the country's severe problems.

It seems to me that the time was ripe for someone like Hitler, who was able to mesmerize the German people into believing that he was their saviour.

I do not remember my father sharing his views on the economic conditions leading up to 1933 with

The Wandervogel – agroup of whom are seen here on an outing – together with the Bündische Jugend were referred to as the German Youth Movement. The National Socialists borrowed much from the Wandervrvogoegel, but then outlawed the groups in 1933.

me. He was more forthcoming about the political situation.

The following events and incidents are an indication of my father's attitude towards the rise of Nazism at the time:

After his return from the war, he completed his degree in architecture, and started working for an architectural firm. He became a member of a union and along with close friends shared social democratic ideals. But most of his life continued to revolve around the Wandervogel youth movement, which he had joined at a very young age, and which played a crucial role in his life before and after the First World War. He devoted his energy to rebuilding Ludwigstein Castle, which was initially dedicated to the memory of those Wandervogel who had been killed during the First World War. Die Burg became a gathering place for like-minded young men and women. My father rose to a leadership position, but resigned in 1930 because he was convinced that the new governor of the province of Hesse was imposing 'fascist tactics' in his efforts to bring the Wandervogel under the wing of the provincial government.

Around that time, my father's first marriage began to unravel. He received a scholarship from the SPD and enrolled at the Goethe University in Frankfurt.

Was there the general feeling that Hitler was the only man who could solve the nation's problems?

Again, I don't know about a general feeling, but here is what I do know:

My mother told me after the Second World War that she believed at the time that a Hitler government would not last any longer than any of the Weimar Republic Governments had. However, what many had hoped for was that Hitler's plan to get people back to work would be realized.

By chance, my parents happened to see Hitler at a small airfield as he was getting off a plane. Their reaction: 'Wir haben uns nichts dabei gedacht.' [We thought nothing of it.]

What were their initial impressions on hearing of the growing popularity of the Nazi party?

Even if the Nazis prevail over the communists in their battle over the power to rule, the Nazis aren't going to last any longer than any of the Weimar Republic governments have since the First World War.

When did you and your family become aware that the Nazis posed a serious threat to a civilized way of life in Germany?

There were many indications during the period leading up to the outbreak of the Second World War. The Nazis curtailed civil liberties, persecuted and imprisoned those whom they considered enemies of the state. Some of my parents' best Wandervogel friends were among them.

But for my father the biggest shock came when he

arrived in Poland in 1941, where he was confronted by the brutal persecution of Jews and Poles.

What was the attitude of your friends, classmates and neighbours to Hitler and the Nazis in the beginning and, if they were devout believers, did they alter their opinion to any degree before, during or after the war?

In first and second grade, my friends and I never talked about politics. Indoctrination was relatively subtle. But, I did overhear adults talking about a man named Hitler, who was getting us into trouble. Officials scolded me for not greeting them with 'Heil Hitler!'

After we moved to Poland, the indoctrination became more intense, especially in high school. All of my classmates appeared to be enthusiastic supporters of Nazism, and if they weren't, they certainly would not have talked about it.

I had one friend whose father was the director of our elementary school. He was an 'old Nazi', and when Herr Direktor Helms objected to the brutal treatment of Jews, he was tried, drafted, ordered to join a suicide squad and was killed at the Russian front shortly thereafter. I did not know what the parents of my other friends thought, and since we lived on the outskirts of town, we had no neighbours.

Even when it became clear that we were going to lose the war, the subject was taboo among my classmates and among most adults.

My parents and their friends voiced their opinions only in hushed tones. My siblings and I were warned not to mention to anyone what we overheard or witnessed.

My general impression was that there were many people who were glad when the war was over, but there were others who had trouble dealing with the fact that Germany had lost the war and that the 1,000-year Reich had collapsed.

Uppermost in everyone's mind was to forget all about the war and to switch into survival mode.

At what point did their unqualified approval of Hitler become tinged with criticism, or did they express a sense of betrayal of the trust the German people had placed in him? Did they blame the Allies for the destruction and privations you shared, or did they acknowledge that the Nazis had brought the destruction of Germany upon themselves?

The thought of whom to blame must have occurred to them. But I'm not sure what the general public thought and felt. People were in shock, they were starving, their cities had been destroyed, they had lost family members, their men had died in battle, gone missing, were maimed or taken prisoner. Millions were uprooted and roamed the countryside looking for shelter and sustenance.

I DO know that they blamed the Allies for the destruction of their cities and the deaths of innocents due to firebombing (in Dresden).

The treatment by French and British occupation

*forces of the German population was severe
compared to that of the Americans (called 'Amis').
We were grateful that we were in the American Zone.
Fear of Russian brutality was widespread. How many
people even considered that it was their revenge for
the atrocities the Nazis visited upon their homeland,
I don't know. But I do not know how many acknowledged that they had brought it upon themselves by
supporting Nazism.*

*There were exceptions: on my website,
www.eyckestrickland.com, I cite an excellent source:*

Wilm Hosenfeld, Ich versuche jeden zu retten: Das
Leben eines deutschen Offizers in Briefen und
Tagebüchern.

*Here was a man who in his diary and letters dealt
with the guilt the German people had to carry.*

*To my knowledge, the news about Nazi atrocities
and the wholesale slaughter of millions in concentration camps began to emerge very slowly. It took
years before people started to deal with the issue.
I believe it was called* Vergangenheitsbewältigung
[confronting the past].

*When the war ended, especially young people
felt that they had been betrayed, misled and used.*

What was your response to the endless daily deluge of propaganda through the radio, press and films?

*Nazi propaganda was ingenious and very effective,
but also very puzzling. Much of it didn't make any
sense to me. Some of it sounded enticing. Some of it
was downright absurd.*

I have discussed my reactions to propaganda and indoctrination in great detail in my memoir.

Did you have the impression that those you knew believed everything they were told by the Nazi leadership?

I'm sure that there were many, but not all, who did. My high school classmates certainly believed everything they were being told. If there were any who didn't, they would not have dared to talk about it.

When did you realize that the rumours of Nazi persecution of those deemed to be enemies of the state were not merely rumours?

It was when one of my brothers observed a death march and the killing of an old Jewish Oma [grandmother]; when I heard the wailing of imprisoned Jewish families; when a boy asked my friend and me to join him at the public hanging for Jews; and when I overheard Frieda Weichmann tell my mother about the Jews 'being taken'.

More descriptions are in my memoir.

How did your father and mother explain why it was important to do all they could to save others when it meant risking their own lives and yours? What was it in their nature that was so lacking in others in that place at that time?

My parents did NOT explain anything nor ask our opinion about their rescue activities at the time. It would have been much too dangerous for us to know. It took many decades before they shared those events with us and even longer before my father decided to talk publicly about his rescue activities, and ONLY after a Wandervogel friend of the family urged him to do so. She and her husband had been members of the SPD. Her husband was imprisoned and killed during a bombing raid while engaged in forced labour.

According to professor of sociology Nechama Tec at the University of Connecticut, there is a set of interdependent characteristics and conditions that Holocaust rescuers share among them, which is the fact that they don't blend into their communities and they are independent people – and they know it. I think these best describe the nature of those who are willing to risk their lives to save others.

You have said that your father did not plan to save Jews but felt compelled to do so out of a sense of responsibility for his fellow men. Why do you think that this same sense of humanity did not compel others?

As described in Nechama Tec's academic paper 'Characteristics and Conditions Rescuers Share', it was nothing 'new or special' that made rescuers like my father decide to help the Jews and Poles who were being persecuted. My father had a history of helping others and so did my mother, albeit in a quiet, less dramatic way. If you read my memoir, you will see that my mother deserves as much credit as my father does.

In 1941, when my father became acquainted with the Weichmann family, and they informed him about the plight of the Jews, he began helping them and countless others.

He did not think of himself as a hero. In a letter to Bundespräsident Gustav Heinemann, he wrote, 'My activities during those tragic and dangerous years were for me (and my wife) only a natural act of humanness and Christian duty! Therefore, basically nothing special! It is an indisputable fact that not all Germans were passive witnesses to the Nazi terror. It was absolutely possible to resist, if one had the will and the ability to do so.'

It is entirely possible that there were many more Germans who hid and aided Jews during the Third Reich, but the sad fact remains that there are only 533 German citizens who are on record as having risked their lives and who were designated as 'Righteous Gentiles', my father, Karl Laabs, being one of the few.

You mentioned the officious types whom your father confounded with bluster and bravado, the nobodies who had been empowered by Hitler with responsibility they would never have been given in normal times. But there were also many intelligent people who succumbed to Nazi ideology. What was your impression of those people and can you explain why they too were converted to Nazism?

I have asked myself that question many times, but haven't come up with a simple answer yet. In the end, it only raises more questions for me.

Was it the ideology that attracted them?

Was it ambition, a thirst for power?

Was it their need to dominate and to feel superior to others?

It is likely that they succumbed to Nazi ideology for a lot of other reasons as well.

What would you say to those who deny the Holocaust or who claim that the entire episode has been exaggerated?

First, I would tell them of my own experiences, of what I saw with my own eyes, what I heard with my own ears and what our family experienced in a little town 11 miles from the death camp of Auschwitz.

I would urge them to look at the undeniable evidence reflected in the meticulous records kept by the Nazis themselves.

I would ask them to open their eyes to the photographs and film footage taken by the Nazis and to those taken at the time of liberation.

I would ask them to open their ears to the stories of survivors collected by Stephen Spielberg as part of his Shoah Visual History Project.

And I would suggest that they listen to the stories of some of the perpetrators, many of whom confessed to having committed unimaginable atrocities.

In the end, if all the evidence does not convince them, nothing will.

I would like to add the following narrative:

In 1948, our family like so many others at that time, were close to starvation. Some of the Jewish survivors who had been rescued by my father had been searching for us for some time. When they found us, they were thrilled. When they heard of our plight, Frieda Weichmann arrived with food and clothing.

We lost contact with them in the coming years, but when in 1983 my mother and I went to Israel to plant a tree in my father's honour, I found their addresses. We reunited with two of the sisters in Denver, Colorado, stayed in contact with them until they died and are close to their daughters and their families to this day.

During my first reading in New York, the grandson of one of the women, whose life my father had saved, introduced himself and proclaimed, 'I wouldn't be here if it weren't for Eycke's father.'

Renata Zerner

Like many Berliners, teenager Renata Zerner grew up believing that the capital of the Reich would be immune to Allied air raids. She and others reassured themselves by recalling that British and American bombers would have to fly 150 miles over enemy territory to reach the outskirts of the city, during which time they would be vulnerable to anti-aircraft fire and attack by German fighters. Besides, they had more accessible targets in the industrial Ruhr and near the coast at Hamburg and Lübeck, where the warships were built.

They recalled that Reichsmarschall Goering had given the population his personal guarantee that no enemy aircraft

Berliners believed that the capital would be immune to Allied air raids, and that British and American bombers had more accessible targets in the industrial Ruhr and near the coast.

would get through the air defences. And yet, as early as 1940, Berlin suffered 30 raids and half as many the following year, though only two in 1942. They had all been largely symbolic, offering a morale boost for the British, and the damage had been superficial. When, in January 1943, the city suffered its first daylight raid and 200 people were killed, the inhabitants dismissed it as an anomaly, a show of force, and told themselves that if and when the raids intensified they would be targeting the Reichschancellery and other government ministries in the centre of the city, or the factories and railway yards far from the residential areas. But they were wrong.

That spring Renata was awoken in the night by sirens. She hurriedly pulled on the old clothes she kept for the long wait in the shelter. There was no communal shelter in the area and the subway stations were not as deep as the London Underground, so residents were forced to take refuge in their basements. If there was a direct hit on the five-storey apartment building in the Bayerische Platz, Renata would be buried alive with her sister Jutta and their parents along with the other tenants.

There was no ignoring the siren. Those who remained in their beds were rudely woken by the air-raid warden, a tenant who took his duties very seriously and evidently enjoyed having the authority. He would ring their doorbell until they showed themselves, then treat them to a lecture on their recklessness and lack of consideration for others, specifically himself. It was only when one of the tenants cornered him alone in a dark corridor, slapped him hard across the face and berated him for bullying them that the warden toned it down.

Berliners tend to be rather aloof, but this shared crisis brought the residents together and they began to talk more freely. While 16-year-old Renata played cards in the smaller of two cellar rooms with the other children, the adults remained in the larger room seated on an odd assortment of discarded sofas and chairs that had been salvaged from the attics. The only strangers who took refuge in the shelter were the local taxi drivers who taught the children skat, a card game they were in the habit of playing while waiting for their next customer.

The small airless room contained two bunk beds for the children, but no one could sleep on the rough blankets. In all there were about 20 people crowded into the two low-ceilinged rooms, which were brightly lit with naked bulbs.

Someone had decorated the walls with large posters of grimacing Soviet soldiers, presumably in an effort to remind them that they were fortunate to be under the Führer's protection. But it only added to their anxiety. If they survived the bombing and Berlin fell to the Red Army ... but thinking ahead was counter-productive. The only way to remain sane was to take one day at a time and believe in Goebbels' boast of final victory – which would be won with a new terror weapon that Germany's top scientists were working on at that very moment.

But such promises gave them little comfort as the sharp crack of anti-aircraft batteries grew louder and the low droning of the enemy bombers drew nearer:

'People talked in low voices, but at each blast they flinched and then they stopped talking ... A young woman, trying to overcome her fear, kept playing the solitaire she had started earlier. She dropped a card and listened. But after a moment, she picked it up and continued to play ... Suddenly, there was a whistle, and then a loud bang and the whole building shook. With one violent sweep, the woman playing solitaire pushed her cards off the table and screamed. Cries cut through the air – then stillness. My heart thumped; I could hardly breathe. Terrified, I looked at my mother, and she saw the fear in my eyes. She murmured, her face white and dead-serious, "It's all right; I think the bomb dropped very near us." My father stood up and said, "It must be the house behind us." Though he looked concerned, his voice was steady and calm.'

Renata felt safe when he was with them. Her father was a veteran of the First World War, and was fond of telling his

daughters of the time he had survived an explosion in the
officers' mess hall, which had been hit by a grenade. She
liked to believe that his presence ensured their safety, even
from falling bombs.

When the all-clear finally sounded they all brushed the
plaster and cement dust from their clothes and filed out
down the long narrow corridor into the street:

*'What a sight! The rooftops of most of the houses around
us had been hit by incendiaries, and the unchecked fires
burned like giant torches. A firestorm blazed in the sky that
blew the sparks into the air from rooftop to rooftop and
covered the black sky with a pink cloud.'*

A bomb had demolished a house directly behind them, but
their apartment block had not been hit. There was little
anyone could do but stand and stare at the awful spectacle.
There were no fire engines to be seen or heard. There
were simply too many fires for the district firefighters to
cope with.

No pets were allowed in the shelter, so on returning to
their apartment Renata coaxed their little terrier out from
under a couch where he was shaking with fear and led him
outside:

*'The view was horrifyingly spectacular. Huge flames
reached into the sky everywhere and caused such a storm
as I had never experienced, never could imagine. It
roared and howled. The fire wind tore through my hair,
my eyes began to burn, and the smell of smoke pene-
trated my clothes and skin ... From then on, everything
would be different.'*

Renata's parents were anti-Nazi on principle, although her father, a physician, had been enrolled in the party by his employers, the Berlin Transportation Department, in 1933. However, after he had opened his own private practice he continued to treat his Jewish patients, although as an Aryan he was forbidden to do so, and he sustained a friendship with other opponents of the regime with whom he shared his views. To do so was to risk being overheard by informers, both those employed by the state and those who did so in the hope of ingratiating themselves with the dictatorship. Renata and her sister were warned by her parents to be discreet and not to talk politics with anyone, even with their best friends. Gestapo spies were everywhere. Storekeepers and their employees listened to customers' conversations, janitors watched the activities of their tenants and their visitors, ticket collectors on public transport eavesdropped on travellers and workmen sweeping the leaves in public parks may have been listening to casual conversations.

But even so, talking in public was less risky than sharing one's private thoughts and opinions over the telephone. Even if the phone was not tapped, Renata's parents were worried that it might have been bugged and were in the habit of putting a pillow over it when they were entertaining their 'closest friends' at home. It was rumoured that an employee of the phone company was sent to install a concealed microphone in suspect households under the pretence of checking the receiver and this listening device was capable of picking up conversations even when the phone was not being used. Renata remembers, 'We kept our doors closed and our voices down.'

Dr Zerner and his wife often met their friends on a Sunday afternoon at the Berlin Zoo in a corner where they could be sure of not being overheard:

'I learned from my parents the ability to question, never to trust implicitly those in charge, not to believe the promises made in speeches and never to ignore the atrocious propaganda posters in public places ... this kind of propaganda is designed to cause fear, and people who live in fear of a common enemy can be easily manipulated.'

Even the most innocuous phrases could be perceived as defeatist. Renata's mother was overheard lamenting the needless loss of civilian lives in an air raid and was summoned to the office of the local mayor to explain her remark. She was able to convince him that her use of the word 'kaput' may have implied that their deaths were futile, but that Berliners used that term in a different way from the people of Kassel, where she was now living with her daughter to escape the bombing.

The threat of being overheard did not, however, deter some from having fun at their leader's expense. 'What is Hitler's favourite song?' Answer: *'Ich weiss, es wird einmal ein Wunder geschehen'* [I know that one day a miracle will happen] The song had been made famous by one of Goebbel's favourite movie stars, Zarah Leander. And there was another joke doing the rounds in the last winter of the war: 'Santa Claus complained to his helpers that he was having problems finding presents for the Nazi leaders. Goebbels would be given a sexy blonde doll and Goering a toy aeroplane but there was nothing for the Führer. He had broken everything Santa had ever given him.'

But gallows humour offered only momentary relief from the grim reality of an increasingly desperate situation.

Fear of the Gestapo was very real and the merest suspicion that one might be spreading defeatist rumours would be sufficient reason for arrest.

Dr Zerner was shocked to see one of his patients, a Herr Volkmann, arrive in his consultation room one day shaking from head to foot, his face ashen and his eyes red from lack of sleep. He had just been released by the Gestapo, who had arrested him for making a derisory remark about the regime while he had been waiting in line at the post office. Herr Volkmann couldn't remember making any such remark and swore that he would never make 'political comments' in public. The informer must have mistaken him for someone else, or made the accusation out of spite. His protestations of innocence had finally been accepted as no one had come forward to corroborate the accusation. Nevertheless, Herr Volkmann now feared that he could be re-arrested at any time. But something else had unnerved him. All night he had been subjected to screaming and sobbing from another cell. When he asked the guard about it he was told it was a young boy of 17 who was to be hung for stealing a chicken.

In October 1944, even schoolboys suddenly found them-selves eligible for recruitment in the SS. Dr Zerner told Renata and her mother that the SS had marched into a classroom in Berlin and ordered all of the boys to join up. One of the 17-year-olds was the son of a friend of theirs. Two months after he had been taken, he was killed on the Eastern Front.

In the final weeks of the war, neither age nor infirmity was considered a hindrance. Elderly men and young boys, some as young as 12, were sworn in to the *Volkssturm* and armed with a *Panzerfaust* [bazooka] with which they were expected to halt the Allied invaders. The population of Berlin and the cities in the path of the encroaching Soviet army were living in fear of what the Russians would do in retalia-tion for the atrocities committed by the SS in the east.

Elsewhere, Nazis and non-Nazis alike had learned to live one day at a time. Food had become so scarce that horsemeat was considered a luxury. Now they had no gas, electricity or hot running water. They boiled water for hot drinks and cooked by lighting fires on their balconies, if they were fortunate enough still to be living with a roof over their heads. People walked through rubble-strewn streets to work or to the market in an effort to maintain at least some semblance of normality. The shortest journey could take an hour or more. The most desirable commodity, though, was not food, but news. Every air raid brought more destruction and fresh casualties and often the only source of news of loved ones was word of mouth. Notices were pinned to the walls of shattered buildings informing anyone who wanted to know that the occupant could now be found in such-and-such a street or in the home of another family who had taken him or her in.

Renata kindly agreed to be interviewed for this book.

What had your parents told you about life in Germany prior to Hitler? Was there the general feeling that he was the only man who could solve the nation's problems?

My parents said that the 1920s, the post-First World War years, were tumultuous and difficult and the crime rate was high. The Weimar Republic was weak, and so was Hindenburg, who was old and ineffective. However, my parents often emphasized that there had been a free press and that the arts flourished. Also, going back to earlier times, they often remarked after hearing of an outrageous act committed by the Nazis, '... this could never have happened under the Kaiser'.

What were your parents' initial impressions of the Nazis?

It was obvious to them that in the beginning, almost all Germans were besotted by Hitler, and everywhere Hitler was considered the new, strong leader for Germany. My parents were Social Democrats and they became concerned about their Jewish friends, my father's patients and his Jewish colleagues.

Threats against communists, socialists, Jews, etc. intensified and were escalated by Hitler's speeches. Many Germans, as well as German Jews, assumed that it would all blow over.

Due to my young age, I really remember very little about my parents' attitudes before Hitler became chancellor except that my father would refer to Hitler and his SA troopers as 'rowdies'.

Did support for Hitler and the Nazis decline with the military's reversals of fortunes, or did the population on the whole remain staunchly loyal to the end?

I have no way to guess at even an approximate number of those who turned against the Nazis at various times, but I can say that in general, at the beginning of the war, everyone was excited about Hitler's successful 'Blitzkrieg'. But as the war wore on and people suffered from bombings, loss of lives everywhere, food rationing, etc. the support for the Nazis fell.

Please consider that in a dictatorship no one could openly ask strangers or those one didn't know very well whether or not they supported Hitler. This question could lead to interrogations or incarcerations in a concentration camp. The official opinion was: of course, everyone loved the Führer and things were going well. So why would anyone ask such a question unless he is against National Socialism?

Here is an example of the fear of being denounced:

My parents attended a dinner party given by close friends who were 'Antis', and knowing this, my mother assumed that the other guests were also 'Antis'. That was until a gentleman she had never met came to her, kissed her hand and introduced himself, murmuring 'Partei' (the German word for party). My mother was shocked and thought that he must be connected with the Nazi Party. She went to the other guests one by one and warned them not to say anything politically dangerous until she found the hostess. She asked her why she had invited an official of the party. The hostess laughed and said, 'No, no, he is all right, his name is Partei.'

One can safely assume that there were those who believed in Hitler at first and when things turned sour, they changed their minds. My mother had a good friend who really believed that Hitler meant well, but she made a quick turnaround before the year 1933 ended.

In time, Hitler's popularity did dribble down, bit by bit, but not necessarily because of the innocent victims in the camps. Mostly it was because people had to deal with their own losses, like losing family members in the war or in an air raid, or they had lost all their belongings. There was discontent in the cities that were bombed, and few escaped the bomb-ings, and people were less afraid to make a remark in public; sometimes they burst out in frustration. Unfortunately, there were often people around who still believed in Hitler and they would turn them in. The Gestapo relied on these 'Spitzels', who were self-appointed spies. Then, after the failed assassina-tion attempt on Hitler, the policing became stricter. It became more dangerous, and the more the German troops withdrew, the more dangerous it became. However, somehow one could feel something under-neath, as if people were waiting for the end. After the capitulation at Stalingrad it became clear to many, but not all, that the war was lost.

People generally knew that there were concentra-tion camps, but again, it is impossible to make an estimate of how many knew what really went on in them. The government's explanation was that they were re-education camps for the state's enemies. Some people found out the truth about the disap-pearance of the Jews, anti-Nazis, gypsies, homosex-uals and others. But no one wanted to talk about what they had heard unless they were sure the other person would not turn them in.

The true believers lived in denial till the end. Our landlady and her two daughters in the little town where we lived when the bombings on Berlin increased was one of those who did not give up. After the American troops entered the town, she said excitedly, 'They are only advance troops, our soldiers (the Germans) will beat them back.' One of her daughters was a schoolmate of mine and I knew her pro-Nazi and anti-Semitic utterings well. All three of them were totally devoted to Hitler.

People in Berlin were not what in other places is considered 'neighbourly'. They greeted each other politely in the elevator or on the stairs, but there was no social talk. All that changed with the air raids when everyone went to the shelter in the basement. There we got to know our neighbours.

In the apartment house in Berlin where my family lived were eight individual apartments. Most of the renters were well educated. There was one family, all of whom were pro-Nazi. I became close friends with one of their daughters. We never touched on politics. She was a Hitler Youth leader. I was not in the Hitler Youth, but it did not change our friendship.

I want to stress again how extremely dangerous it was in Nazi Germany to ask strangers, or those one did not know well, whether or not they supported Hitler. However, there was a way to find out, and that was by developing a conversation: a vague remark of concern or by calling Hitler by his name and not 'Führer', and bit by bit one could determine where the other person stood: on the side of the Nazis or anti-Nazis.

The mentality of the Nazis is interesting. In the post-war time the fear continued, but now the tables were turned: it was the pro-Nazi types who feared admitting their pro-Nazi opinions. They thought that they would receive the same punishment that the Nazis had meted out to their political enemies. Consequently, many would not say much about their *past unless it was publicly known, and if they could, they would not admit that they had believed in, or worked for, Hitler.*

When did the unqualified support for the regime begin to crumble?

Again, it is difficult to pinpoint a specific time when the breakdown of the support for Hitler occurred, since a negative political opinion could not be expressed. After the war, much was said about speaking up or having the moral courage to stand up against the regime, but that is naive. Those who did were all killed.

It seems to me that most of the Germans blamed the Allies, certainly in the beginning. Many blamed the German people for not supporting Hitler. Eventually many realized that it had been a bad policy to invade Poland and thus start the war. And there were those who believed in a German victory to the end. For instance, our history teacher corrected us when we spoke of 'after the war'. We were to say 'after our victory'. I assume they blamed the Allies and the anti-Nazis.

Many years later, in the 1970s, a friend who had served as an army nurse in Russia during the war told me that she blamed the loss of the war on the soldiers, and that we could have won if so many of them had not deserted or capitulated. I did not ask her at the time, but I suspect that she had been pro-Hitler.

Again, at the time one could sense an atmosphere of discontent, but not much more. There were complaints about the food rationing, the lack of coal to heat the homes, lack of clothing and more. Of course, there was no gasoline for individuals who owned cars, unless they had a special need like physicians in order to make calls. In the towns and cities, people had little time after spending hours in the air-raid shelter, trying to get to work, which was sometimes impossible, or attempting to find an open food store. It was especially hard for women with young children.

No one said much aloud, but one could tell much from their exhausted looks, from their hasty, nervous manners and obvious frustrations. People from bombed-out cities who came to the small town where we stayed told each other what they had lost: their houses, or all of their belongings in the apartments. In addition, after all that, some received notice that a father, a son or a husband had been killed.

I cannot remember now, but I am sure that at the time there were people who made subtle remarks to indicate that their pro-Nazi feelings turned into feelings of betrayal. I myself feel strongly that Hitler and Nazi Germany had betrayed me and cheated me out of my youth, caused the loss of my father and my future. To know that others had lost and suffered much more never diminished my pain.

How did you insulate yourselves against the continual bombardment of Nazi propaganda?
We discussed radio, press, theatre and film at home at the dinner table. By the time I knew what propaganda was, it did not affect me. Frankly, much of it

was simplistic and stupid, loaded with slogans. I just remember one incident: I was waiting at a streetcar stop and looked at a page of the Völkischer Beobachter *paper that was posted in a glassed-in frame on a stand – obviously it was placed there for people to read while they waited for their ride. On the page was a nasty pornographic drawing of a Jew. I understood the meanness of it and was disgusted.*

The contents of most films with stars like Zarah Leander were filled with propaganda. I was more interested in the stars and their acting abilities than in the propaganda. I believe it came to a point that one did not expect anything else but propaganda. An exception was the comedies, which did not contain propaganda.

What was your impression of the effect propaganda had on your neighbours, friends and fellow students?

Many of those I knew believed everything. However, I never asked my classmates or anyone else if they believed all they were told. It would have been too dangerous. Usually they revealed their full trust, like, for instance, a woman I knew made the ridiculous comment that Hitler would invade England '… when the English Channel freezes over' (I don't know if, after the war, she ever found out the truth!).

There were others who repeated as truth everything they were told on the radio and in the press, but it's difficult to know how many and when doubts set in … if ever. Many of the believers were badly educated, and I assume, not very bright, and much was their wishful thinking. But not all swallowed the garbage that Goebbels dished out, regardless of education.

Some very intelligent people went along with the Nazis, while some uneducated ones were against them. I think it was more a matter of gut feeling.

My family and I did not socialize with devout Nazis. If such an occasion arose, one would make small talk and, if possible, cut the conversation short.

I must have been around nine or ten when my parents discussed these matters in front of us children with the warning never, never to tell others about this 'or we would end up in one of those camps'.

When did you learn of what was happening in the camps?

We had Jewish friends and my father had Jewish patients, who told my parents what was happening. My father's office nurse (she and her family were good friends of my family) had been with us for many years, despite the Nazi prohibition to employ Jews; when it became too dangerous, she left us and later left Germany in 1939, on the day the war broke out. After the war we kept in touch with her, as well as with her surviving sister.

I was only six years old when Hitler came to power. My family was from Berlin, and Berliners in general, but not always, take a different view from the rest of the country. Being a Berliner myself, I like to think that they are perhaps more savvy in regard to politics and often better informed, since they live in close vicinity to the seat of their government and also to political gossip and rumours. What people felt about Hitler and the Nazis differed greatly in various parts of Germany, and varied depending on whether they were in the farm communities or in the cities.

The Bombing of Dresden

By February 1945 the inhabitants of Dresden were hoping that they were past the worst that the war had in store for Germany. They reassured themselves that the city, known as Florence on the Elbe because of its cultural treasures and baroque architecture, had no strategic importance and it could only be a matter of months before hostilities would cease and they could begin to rebuild their lives. But on the night of 13 February the Allies launched the first of four air assaults calculated to obliterate the city, which they considered a legitimate target because of its abundance of factories in the industrial section and its value as a communication and transportation centre.

Over two consecutive nights, 1,250 bombers dropped approximately 4,000 tonnes of high explosives and incendiary devices, turning the city centre into an inferno. The resulting firestorm caused widespread destruction and the deaths of some 25,000 civilians (the figure quoted at the time by the city authorities, which was subsequently verified in 2010, though others have claimed the number of fatalities could be far higher).

One of the survivors, Hannelore Rebstock, relived the horror of those raids in an interview with Professor Tubach of the University of California, author of *German Voices*.

The rubble-strewn streets could make the shortest journey to and from work or school extremely hazardous, and a ten-minute walk could extend to an hour or more.

February is carnival month in Germany and the afternoon of the first air raid had seen children playing in the streets in their fancy-dress costumes, but by nine that evening, when the wireless warned of the approaching bombers, they were all safely inside their homes or tucked up in bed. Hannelore threw herself on the floor of the air-raid shelter when the first bombs fell and the ground heaved underneath her feet. As more bombs fell, the earthen floor rippled with the impact then all was silent. Hannelore and her mother emerged from their underground shelter and surveyed the raging firestorm in the company of their neighbours. It was an indescribable scene and one that has evidently haunted her ever since.

Unknown to the Allies, the population had been increased by 500,000 refugees fleeing the Russian advance, many of whom had converged on the square in front of the main railway station, hoping that they would be guided to the shelters. But the city had not built communal shelters because Dresden Council assumed that it would not be targeted. Consequently, many of these refugees were out in the open when the bombers flew over the railway station, which was a prime target.

By the time the second wave dropped their lethal loads, at around midnight, the shocked refugees had been joined by hundreds of shell-shocked residents, who had emerged from their shelters to appraise the damage. Tragically, no warning of the second raid could be given as the alarms had been knocked out earlier that evening. Hannelore survived, but she was scarred by her experience, particularly the days she spent digging through the rubble to recover dead bodies, traumatized by the sight of what she had initially thought were tree stumps, but which turned out to be the charred and distorted remains of her fellow citizens.

It was too disturbing to comprehend. She was in shock for weeks and suffered nightmares for many years afterwards. She and her fellow survivors became numb, 'dead and rigid inside'. Even while they stood side by side clearing the rubble, brick by brick, they did so in complete silence and never talked about their experience.

Anneliese Heider

During the 1930s, Anneliese Heider and her elder brother Ludwig enjoyed a typical upper-middle-class childhood in a suburb of Munich, one that offered them a singular glimpse of life in Hitler's Reich, for the Bavarian capital was the birthplace of National Socialism. Their father, Martl, a disabled veteran of the Great War, had worked as a carpenter for the railway before 1914 and on his return he was employed as a clerk. Their mother, Elisabeth, had been a cook and when food prices went sky-high in the early 1920s she still managed to feed her family by buying the less expensive offal and beef bones to make nourishing dishes.

Even after the couple had managed to save enough to purchase their newly built two-storey stucco house, they continued to live frugally, as if every pfennig counted. Martl built and repaired much of their furniture, sharpened the kitchen utensils and was proud of the fact that he wouldn't throw away a bent nail if he could straighten it and use it again. Elisabeth owned only two dresses, repaired the family's clothes and made her own pickles and preserves, which were kept in the coldest part of the hall, as fridges and freezers were a prohibitively expensive luxury.

The entire house could be warmed by a single anthracite stove, although each room had a small tiled stove that was used only when the weather was especially cold. The basement contained their father's workshop, the storeroom for fruit, vegetables and jars of homemade quince and apple sauce, jelly and jam. Here, too, was the laundry room where the monthly washing was soaked in a large boiling cauldron and scrubbed on a long wooden table. The wet linen was then rinsed in large tubs and wrung out by hand. If the weather was good, the damp items were hung outside to air and if not, they would be carried up to the attic where they could dry overnight.

It was an idyllic time for Anneliese with spring and

summer evenings spent playing alongside her parents in the garden, Sunday outings to the forest, visits to the circus and an annual trip to the Christkindlmarkt in Munich's Marienplatz. By the time that Anneliese was ten, she particularly enjoyed travelling into the city with her mother to shop at the big department stores. However, in November 1938 they were turned away from their favourite store, Tietz, by two brown-shirted SA men who told them, 'Germans don't shop in Jewish stores.' Anneliese was troubled, not only by the threatening presence of the SA, but also by her mother's failure to assert herself. It was unsettling to see that the people who had been turned away from Tietz had crowded into the next store and there was a long queue for the restaurant. It seemed that everyone was allowing themselves to be ordered around by the two thugs. In religion class she had been told that God loves everyone and that Jesus was a Jew. What had happened to turn her churchgoing mother and her neighbours into obedient sheep?

At elementary school the crucifix was exchanged for a framed photo of the Führer and the morning prayer was replaced by an obligatory 'Heil Hitler!' More worryingly, she was haunted by the fear of what might have happened to her new 'Sunday' friend Franz, a disabled boy who visited them one Sunday each month under an arrangement made through their church. After many happy visits during the summer and autumn of 1938, Franz suddenly stopped coming to their home and no explanation was offered. The next spring, Martl was told that Franz had been sent to a special clinic for treatment. Some time after that his family was notified that he had died of natural causes and his body cremated so that it could not be returned for burial. Two years later, in 1941, the Nazi's euthanasia programme was exposed by Bishop Galen and although the priests who printed and distributed the bishop's sermons were arrested and executed, the public outcry was sufficient to force Hitler to order it to be ended.

The war saw Ludwig drafted into the observer corps and their garden given over to growing potatoes and vegetables. As the war dragged on and rationing restricted every necessity from soap to darning thread, more of their flower beds were sacrificed for essential produce. Local produce wasn't rationed because it would spoil if not sold while fresh, but the long queues at the grocers forced many families to grow their own. Apples and pears were plentiful, but oranges and other citrus fruits were rare as they had to be imported.

German bureaucracy reached new heights of absurdity under National Socialism. Families were allowed to keep one and a half chickens per person, but these had to be registered and if a chicken died or was killed for the pot, its severed head had to be produced to prove it was no longer capable of producing eggs. If more hens were kept than the law permitted, their eggs had to be handed over to a distribution centre. Firewood became scarce but the authorities prohibited the cutting of trees or the lopping of branches, so the Heiders and their neighbours took to foraging in the woods for fallen branches after a storm. With coal a scarcity, Martl swallowed his pride and went scavenging by the railway for pieces of coal that might have fallen from the coal wagons.

Even the quality of the food changed during the war. Full-cream milk was replaced by a thin, watery concoction with a distinct blue tinge and saccharin replaced sugar. Like many Münchners, the Heider family began foraging in the woods for whatever edibles they could find. Mushrooms became a staple ingredient, but there were other sources of nourishment that served as replacements for foodstuffs and ingredients they could no longer buy. *Fichtennadelhonig* was made from the sticky new shoots of the fir tree when honey was unobtainable, and cakes had to be made with hot water and eggs as there was no fat.

Restaurants, cafés, bierkellers and hotels were also subject to rationing. Two days a week they had to provide meals without meat, and once a month many local eateries would offer a serving of vegetable stew with scraps of meat donated by the local butcher as part of *Eintopf Sonntag* [one-pot Sunday], for which customers didn't need to use up their precious ration coupons.

Anneliese confessed that what she had once considered to be necessities before the war had now become unobtainable luxuries and they had to do without them. But for children of her age there were unexpected diversions. Class would be cancelled for the morning while the children were marched to a nearby farm to pick the harmful brown-and-yellow-striped bugs from the potato plants, or harvest the crops after the farm labourers had been drafted into the armed forces. Education was no longer the priority. One of her cousins had been sent to a private school north of the city, but the students there too were excused class and sent to a hop farm where they picked hops for the breweries five days a week, returning home only at weekends.

As a member of the BDM, Anneliese was required to complete a first-aid course and her mother enrolled too, as it was evident that the population of Munich and every other town and city could no longer rely on the availability of ambulances or medical personnel after the Allied air raids intensified. And when their class finished for the day they were expected to remain and roll bandages for the front.

In the autumn of 1941, every civilian was issued with a gas mask and compelled to practise wearing it for minutes at a time. They were tight and smelled strongly of rubber. Even Christmas had to be diminished to allow for wartime restrictions. The Heider Christmas tree had been an annual delight, stretching to the ceiling, but from 1941 the family had to be content with a miniature version that stood on a table due to the potential fire hazard if the house were to be hit during an air-raid.

Despite Reichsmarschall Goering's boast that his Luftwaffe would stop enemy aircraft from bombing German towns and cities, the Allied air raids intensified through the winter of 1942–3. The Americans bombed by day and the British by night. Consequently, civilians had to be prepared to stop whatever they were doing at a moment's notice and take to the shelters. The Heider family sheltered in their own basement and made it as safe as they could from flying shrapnel and incendiaries by putting heavy cement blocks over the windows. Each member of the family packed a suitcase with essential items in case they were confined to the basement for several days and, once in the shelter, they turned on the radio to listen to the *Luftlagemeldung*, which broadcast the location of the enemy bombers.

Being in close proximity to the Dornier aircraft factory, the Heiders and their neighbours knew it would be only a matter of time before their district became a target for the Allied planes.

One clear night, the neighbourhood was roused from sleep by the wailing siren and the people rushed to their shelters, where they waited anxiously for the first bombs to fall. The noise was deafening; the ground shook and the doors and windows banged against their frames as if shaken by a fierce wind. They had been left unlocked to prevent them being blown open and causing more damage and injury. Their ordeal seemed to go on for hours but it was no more than a few minutes. However, when the all-clear was finally sounded the survivors emerged to discover that the basement shelters had not been strong enough to save their neighbours. Many houses had collapsed, burying the occupants alive under the rubble. To avoid the same fate, some families decided to build a shelter between the houses. The Heiders dug a deep trench with their neighbour and shored up the sides with timber and the roof with railroad sleepers. Several feet of sand was shovelled in on top to diffuse incendiaries and the floor was lined with old rugs. It was then stocked with water, torches, first-aid equipment, candles, tinned food and plenty of thick blankets as it was unheated. It wouldn't have been able to withstand a direct hit, but it was sturdy enough to deflect shrapnel and flying debris and that was the best they could hope for.

But still life had to go on and the population took their pleasures as and when they could. For her Christmas present that year, Anneliese persuaded her parents to allow her to go on a short skiing holiday with a friend to Garmisch, where the 1936 Winter Olympics had taken place. But even there the war was still within sight as Anneliese saw to her horror one night when Munich came under attack from Allied planes. Few homes had telephones at that time so she could only watch in shocked silence and pray that her parents were safe while the sky was lit by a fearful firework display.

When the Allies intensified their raids in January 1943, they began to use flares to guide the bombers to their targets. These lit the sky so brightly that it was possible to read a newspaper even though the city was in a total blackout. Although the military targets were now hit with more accuracy, there was still considerable collateral damage, including civilian homes, so survivors had to be rehoused. The Heider home was requisitioned for evacuees, although it turned out that these were a baroness and her daughter who had been bombed out of their palatial home in Hamburg. Having had servants to tend to their every need, they had no idea how to clean the two rooms assigned to them or cook even the most basic meals and had to ask their reluctant hostess how to do the simplest chores.

The homeless aristocrats made no concessions to their new situation, and many saw no reason why they shouldn't wear their jewellery around the house and even in the air-raid shelter.

As Anneliese grew into young adulthood she found the restrictions and wartime conditions more difficult to accept than she had as a child. She realized there were few young men to date as all but the youngest had been drafted and there were no dances to go to as public dances had been prohibited for some time. Any socializing had to be done when the weather was bad and there was less likelihood of an air raid. If fine weather and clear skies were forecast, one stayed home and waited anxiously for the siren. If the sky was overcast and there was heavy rain, it was a good time to go out to the cinema, restaurant, café or to visit friends. Daily life was turned inside out.

People dealt with the rapidly worsening situation in different ways and despite the ever-present threat of the informer, many couldn't resist a joke at the leadership's expense.

The following was typical: 'Have you heard the Swiss have

appointed a minister of the navy and they don't even have a port?' Answer: 'Well, we have a minister of justice—'

Then there was the joke about the man who showed his friend his new car. When they looked under the bonnet there was no engine. The proud owner explained, 'It's OK. I never travel to foreign countries and in Germany it's all downhill anyway.'

In March 1944, at the age of 16, Anneliese graduated and went to work in the railway administration offices where her father was employed. There she befriended other girls in the secretarial department and discovered that the war imposed further difficulties and regulations. When the air-raid siren sounded, every girl had to carry her typewriter down to the basement shelter as these were hard to replace. Just before one particular raid, several young women who were tired of carrying their typewriters up and down the stairs decided to take the elevator. Their bodies were never found.

There were 70 air-raids on Munich that year, each carried out by several hundred bombers. Few buildings escaped damage and almost every inhabitant suffered the loss of either their home, their loved ones or their friends. Some experienced all of these, but life went on.

Anneliese has given a graphic account of what it was like to be in the midst of air attack at work in her biography *Christmas Trees Lit the Sky*.

As she describes it, people were still on their way down to the basement when a bomb hit the building. As soon as the noise of the blast subsided, the air was filled with the cries and moaning of the injured and the dying. Concrete dust choked the air and rubble blocked the entrance to the shelter. There appeared to be no way out. The young secretaries clung to each other in panic, but couldn't stop themselves from shaking. Someone could be heard praying amid the pitiable moaning of the injured. More bombs struck the building and the girls looked up at the ceiling, praying that it wouldn't come down on top of them. Between the awful whistling and the impact, people could be heard calling for medics and for men to help extinguish fires that were raging on the upper floors. The girls dampened their handkerchiefs in the water buckets and pressed them to their mouths and noses so that they could breathe. Finally, the all-clear sounded and they stumbled out through a connecting door to another shelter, blindly following the person in front until they came to an emergency exit.

Outside there were hundreds of people scrambling through the rubble, searching for friends and colleagues or simply milling about in a daze.

Buildings were burning and many roads were impassable as Anneliese started the long walk home. There were no trams or trains and no familiar landmarks to tell her where she was or the direction in which she was heading. All she knew was that she had to get away from that dreadful scene. She negotiated bomb craters and walked gingerly between fallen power lines. And all the time she was trying to choke back the fear that her father had been killed and she would never see him again.

Every now and then a solitary car or small truck passed loaded with people but none stopped for her. Eventually, after what seemed like hours, she was offered a lift by the driver of a truck, who told her he was going as far as Passing, which was close to where she lived. There she was left to walk the last few kilometres past the burnt-out shells of street cars and their passengers, who would not be coming home.

Though by now she was exhausted, once she turned into her street and saw that the house was still standing she found herself running towards it, her heart pounding, tears streaming down her face. Her mother opened the door. Her father was there too. They were all safe.

Miraculously, the Heider family saw out the end of the war in that same house, unharmed by the destruction that had raged around them.

Above and previous page: The damage inflicted on German towns and cities by the first Allied air-raids did not appear to demoralize a people conditioned to expect ultimate victory, but as the raids intensified many began to doubt the propaganda.

Aftermath

After the war, Germany was invited to participate in an international cultural event, but those responsible for selecting the programme could not decide which song or piece of music would be suitable for them to perform. The German national anthem was out of the question because of its association with the Nazis, while Beethoven's 'Ode to Joy' was considered inappropriate under the circumstances. It was finally decided that the singers would perform an old folk tune, '*O du lieber Augustin*', which tells of a drunkard falling into a plague pit and emerging unharmed and untroubled by his traumatic experience thanks to the numbing effects of the alcohol. It seemed a fitting choice.

'The man who founded the Third Reich, who ruled it ruthlessly and often with uncommon shrewdness, who led it to such dizzy heights and to such a sorry end, was a person of undoubted, if evil, genius. It is true that he found in the German people, as a mysterious Providence and centuries of experience had moulded them up to that

time, a natural instrument which he was able to shape to his own sinister ends.'

(William L. Shirer, *The Rise and Fall of teh Third Reich: A History of Nazi Germany*)

Bibliography

Barnett, Victoria, *For the Soul of the People* (Oxford University Press, 1998)

Berger, Thomas, *Lebenssituationen unter der Herrschaft des Nationalsozialismus* (Hannover, 1981)

Bielenberg, Christabel, *The Past is Myself* (Corgi, 1988)

Engelmann, Bernt, *In Hitler's Germany* (Schocken, 1992)

Heider Tisdale, Anneliese, *Christmas Trees Lit the Sky* (AuthorHouse, 2012)

Hitler, Adolf, *Mein Kampf* (Jaico, 2007)

Hoffmann, Peter, *The History of the German Resistance 1933–1945* (McGill Queen's University Press, 1996)

Hosenfeld, Wilm, *Ich versuche jeden zu retten: Das Leben eines deutschen Offiziers in Briefen und Tagebüchern.* Militärgschichtliches Forschungsamt, ed. Thomas Vogel (Deutsche Verlagsanstalt, München, 2004)

Kruger, Horst, *A Crack in the Wall: Growing Up Under Hitler* (Fromm International, 1966)

Large, David Clay, *Nazi Games: The Olympics of 1936* (W.W. Norton, 2007)

Massaquoi, Hans-Jürgen, *Destined to Witness: Growing Up Black in Nazi Germany* (Harper Collins, 2009)

Mayer, Milton, *They Thought They were Free* (University of Chicago Press, 2013)

McKee, Ilse, *Tomorrow the World* (J.M. Dent and Sons, 1960)

Moorhouse, Roger, *Berlin at War: Life and Death in Hitler's Capital, 1939–45* (Vintage, 2011)

Roland, Paul, *The Nuremberg Trials: The Nazis and Their Crimes Against Humanity* (Arcturus, 2012)

Roland, Paul, *Nazi Women: The Attraction of Evil* (Arcturus, 2014)

Schönhaus, Cioma, *The Forger* (Granta, 2008)

Shirer, William L., *The Rise and Fall of teh Third Reich: A History of Nazi Germany* (Arrow, 1991)

Shirer, William L., *Berlin Diary* (Sunburst, 1997)

Shirer, William L., *The Nightmare Years, 1930–1940* (Little Brown, 1984)

Strickland, Eycke, *Eyes are Watching, Ears are Listening: Growing Up in Nazi Germany, 1933–1946.* A Memoir by Eycke Strickland (iUniverse, 2008)

Tubach, Frederic C., *German Voices* (University of California Press, 2011)

Vaizey, Hester, *Surviving Hitler's War: Family Life in Germany: 1939–48* (Palgrave, 2010)

Resources

Transdiffusion.org

Return2style.de

tikkun.org

historynet.org

theguardian.com/uk

rijo.homepage.t-online.de

nptelegraph.com

eyckestrickland.com

renatazerner.com

'The Nazis: A Warning from History' (BBC, 1997)

'The World At War – Inside The Reich' (ITV, 1973–4)

Index

Index

Index

illegitimacy 118–19
informers
  use of 91–3

Jacobs, Helene
  experience in school 22
jazz
  Nazi disapproval of 63–4
  and swing kids 66–7
Jud Süss 103
Jungvolk 54, 56

K., Beate 121–2
Kastner, Erich x
Kauffmann, Herr 115
Keitel, Wilhelm 95
Keller, Helen 30, 32
Kindertransport 51
Klemperer, Victor
  on Berlin Olympics 74
Kreisleiter 91
Kristallnacht 48–50, 97–101
Kruger, Horst
  and popularity of Hitler 12, 14, 15, 17
Kulle, Herr 91–3

Laabs, Auguste 125, 126, 137
Laabs, Karl
  opposition to Nazi Germany 125, 126,
    127, 128–9, 131, 132, 134, 137–9,
    140
Labour Service 14
Law for the Organization of National
  Labour (1934) 26–7
Law for the Prevention of Hereditarily
  Diseased Offspring (1933) 40
Law for the Protection of the
  Hereditary Health of the German
  People (1935) 40–1
League of German Girls (BDM) 38, 47,
  57, 59–60
Leander, Zarah 146, 155
Levy, Dr 7, 8
Ley, Robert 27

suicide of ix
  on Nazi control of populace 52
  and moral self-mutilation 94
Lindbergh, Charles 76
Lippe 11–12
Lloyd George, David 71
London, Jack 30
Long, Luz 77
Louis, Joe 70
Ludendorff, General 3

Mann, Thomas 30
Marga's
  childhood of 9–10
Massaquoi, Hans-Jürgen
  childhood of 69–70
Mayer, Helene 79
Mayer, Milton 24, 25
McKee, Ilse in League of German Girls
  55, 59–60
media
  control of 101–3
Mein Kampf (Hitler) 30, 39, 43, 46, 54
Mengele, Josef ix
moral self-mutilation 93–5
Munich Beer Hall Putsch 4, 47
Myth of the Twentieth Century, The
  (Rosenberg) 45–6

National Socialist Women's Organiza
  tion 18
Nazi Party
  reasons for joining xi, 1–2
  rise of 2–4, 6, 129, 131
  Bernt Engelmann witnesses rise of
    6–9, 10
  takes power 11–12
  view of women 18–19
  leaders' behaviour 19–20, 90
  loyalty to 20–1
  alignment of institutions to 21–5,
    29–30
  rigging of elections 60–1
  disapproval of swing kids 63–8
  public support for 96

Picture Credits

Corbis: viii (Bettmann), 5 (Bettmann), 13 (Bettmann), 31 (Bettmann), 43 (Austrian Archives), 56 (Stapleton Collection), 58 (Underwood & Underwood), 66 (Underwood & Underwood), 71 (Bettmann), 77 (Bettmann), 83 (Berliner Verlag/Archiv/dpa), 88 (Hulton-Deutsch Collection), 92 (Bettmann), 99 (Bettmann)

Getty Images: 2 Three Lions/Stringer), 16 (ullstein bild), 28 (FPG), 34 (Alfred Eisenstaedt), 39 (ullstein bild), 49 (Mondadori), 122 (ullstein bild), 130 (ullstein bild), 141 (Keystone-France), 158 (ullstein bild), 169 (Arkady Shaikhet), 170 (ullstein bild)

Kobal Collection: 118 (UFA)

Shutterstock: 107 (Everett Historical)

Topfoto: 35 (ullstein bild)